Essential Business Law and Practice for SQE1

Bill Davies
with contributions from
Rachel Cooper

Routledge
Taylor & Francis Group
LONDON AND NEW YORK

Designed cover image: amtitus / Getty Images

First published 2023
by Routledge
4 Park Square, Milton Park, Abingdon, Oxon OX14 4RN

and by Routledge
605 Third Avenue, New York, NY 10158

Routledge is an imprint of the Taylor & Francis Group, an informa business

British Library Cataloguing-in-Publication Data
A catalogue record for this book is available from the British Library

ISBN: 978-1-032-26754-8 (hbk)
ISBN: 978-1-032-26753-1 (pbk)
ISBN: 978-1-003-28976-0 (ebk)

DOI: 10.4324/9781003289760

Typeset in The Sans
by Deanta Global Publishing Services, Chennai, India

Access the SQE Companion Website here: www.routledge.com/cw/sqe

Essential Business Law and Practice for SQE1

Essential Business Law and Practice for SQE1 explains the key principles of business law and practice as required for the Solicitors Qualifying Examination (SQE) Part 1, in a clear, easy-to-follow style.

The key principles of law in each topic are introduced together with concise examples of how each principle can be applied, and the book includes a range of supporting features:

- Commercial awareness talking points reinforce the book's strong focus on commercial awareness throughout.
- Multiple-choice questions: Each section of the book provides multiple-choice questions following the SQE1 question format (with answers to enable you to test your knowledge). Further multiple-choice questions and answers are also provided on the companion website.
- Problem questions: To test understanding and analytical skills applied to practical scenarios. A companion website also provides suggested answers.
- Revision points: Each chapter concludes with a concise list of key revision points.

Part of Routledge's Essential Law for SQE1 series, this concise and accessible text provides a clear understanding of the business law and practice element of SQE1 and enables you to test your assessment skills. Without the assumption of any prior knowledge of Business Law and Practice, it is suitable for non-law graduates.

Bill Davies is Dean of the Faculty of Law, Crime and Justice at University of Winchester. He teaches company and commercial law.

Rachel Cooper is Course Leader for undergraduate Accounting and Finance courses at the University of Worcester. She teaches management accounting and strategy.

Essential Law for SQE1

Essential Law for SQE1
Series editor: Wendy Laws

Essential Law for SQE1 is a series of concise textbooks aligned to the latest SQE1 curriculum. Providing candidates with an accessible summary of the core principles in each area of law, the style of each book is precise, with bullet-point lists summarizing key information and revision points concluding each chapter. The books also feature multiple choice questions with answers, example problem questions and a glossary of key cases.

For more information about this series, please visit: www.routledge.com/

Essential Tort Law for SQE1
Wendy Laws

Essential Dispute Resolution for SQE1
Ben Waters

Essential Business Law and Practice for SQE1
Bill Davies

Contents

Introduction

The aim of the book is to provide a clear explanation of the key principles of Business Law and Practice required for the **Solicitors Qualifying Examination Part 1 Functioning Legal Knowledge** ("SQE 1").[1]

The design of the book has been influenced by the nature and content of the SQE1 assessment. In particular:

- SQE1 consists solely of 360 multiple-choice questions that are sat over two closed-book examinations. Business Law and Practice (BLP) is one of 14 subject areas assessed.
- SQE1 is designed to test the knowledge and application expected of a newly qualified solicitor.
- The exam does not require knowledge of case names or statutes, except in cases where the name of the case or statute is essential to express the law. For example, *the Rule in Rylands v Fletcher.*
- The SQE1 is designed to assess the law as it stands at the date of the examination. It does not assess the historical development of the law or its potential development.
- The BLP syllabus covers areas of business law and practice including those that currently feature in many LLB company law modules.
- The syllabus focuses mainly on four types of business organisations: sole traders, partnerships, limited liability partnerships, and private companies limited by share. Although public limited companies are referred to, the law, governance, and regulation of publicly listed companies do not feature in the syllabus.
- Although not explicitly stated in the curriculum, answering any problem-based BLP scenarios often requires students to demonstrate a contextual understanding of how businesses operate. This can sometimes be described as demonstrating "commercial awareness".
- Based on the above, this book systematically covers the content of the BLP syllabus in a clear and accessible way. The key principles of law in each topic are introduced together with concise examples of how each principle can be

1 See: SQE1 Functioning Legal Knowledge Assessment Specification, updated 14 October 2020, published by the Solicitors Regulation Authority, available via www.sra.org.uk.

applied. There is a strong focus on commercial awareness throughout the book and most chapters contain a signposted "commercial awareness talking point". Application of the law in practice through multiple-choice questions is featured in Chapters 19 and 21.

- The book does not assume any prior knowledge of Business Law and Practice and is written on the understanding that readers may also be non-law graduates.
- Reflecting the nature of the SQE, the book does not consider the historical development of law through cases or statute, nor does it focus on the potential future development of the law, unless this impacts on aspects of commercial awareness.
- Where appropriate and necessary, cases and statutes are referenced, but detailed case analysis and legal research are not a feature as the book is focused on the requirements of SQE1.

Solicitors Qualifying Examination – SQE 1

This book covers the areas of Business Law and Practice in the **SQE 1** assessment specification:

- Business and organisational characteristics (sole trader/partnership/LLP/private and unlisted public companies).
- Legal personality and limited liability.
- Formation of a company/partnership/LLP.
- Corporate governance and compliance.
- Partnership decision-making and authority of partners.
- Insolvency (corporate and personal).
- Business taxation.

Key features to assist learning

Revision points: Each chapter concludes with a concise list of key revision points.

Multiple-choice questions: The SQE 1 assessment uses multiple-choice questions to test understanding of key principles. Multiple-choice questions, following the SQE format, are provided in Chapter 19 of the book and answers are provided in Chapter 20.

Commercial awareness: Most chapters contain commercial-awareness talking points that encourage students to contextualise their learning.

Problem scenarios: Problem scenarios are provided in Chapter 21, to enable readers to test their understanding and their client case analysis skills. These scenarios are informed by the style and substance of those that can be expected on the SQE2. Suggested answers are available at www.routledge.com/cw/sqe.

The law is stated as of 13 July 2022.

PART 1

Choosing a business form

1 Business organisations

1.1 Chapter overview

Solicitors are often required to give advice on which business forms are appropriate for a client's needs. To advise on business forms, a knowledge of the key features of different business forms is essential. Of particular importance is a knowledge of important concepts such as limited liability and separate legal personality which are features of a number of business forms. These concepts, discussed in more detail in Chapter 2, can combine to enable businesspeople to protect themselves if the business fails by limiting their liability to the debts of the business and preventing creditors from suing for their personal assets. Despite these advantages, a limited liability organisation may still not be the most suitable. The appropriate business form will depend on factors such as the client's attitude to risk and the nature, size, and complexity of the business.

This chapter considers the types of business organisations that are listed in the curriculum of the Solicitors Qualifying Examination: Sole traders, ordinary partnerships, limited liability partnerships, private limited companies, and public limited companies.

1.2 Sole traders

This is the most straightforward type of business organisation and the most common form operating in the UK today. Sole traders are individual people who are self-employed. They are human beings rather than corporate forms. Many of the companies and partnerships in the UK today originated as sole traderships.

Being a sole trader is often much less administratively burdensome than other business organisations and can be the most cost-effective way for a business to operate. If the business fails, sole traders are liable for any outstanding debts as they have unlimited liability. This means that if the business fails, the sole trader may have to pay debts from personal assets.

DOI: 10.4324/9781003289760-2

Sole traders are treated as individuals by the tax system and are liable to pay income tax on profits. Sole traderships are not registered at Companies House but sole traders do need to register with Her Majesty's Revenue & Customs (HMRC) as self-employed.

Some solicitors operate as sole traders, usually referred to as sole practitioners.

1.3 Ordinary partnerships

The definition of a partnership comes from the Partnership Act 1890 (PA 1890): "The relation which subsists between persons carrying on a business in common with a view of profit."[1]

Ordinary partnerships can arise very informally and do not require a written partnership agreement, although one is nearly always advisable. Unless the partners contract otherwise in an agreement, the default rules in the PA 1890 will apply.

There is no requirement for ordinary partnerships to be registered at Companies House and, consequently, the running of a partnership will usually be much less administratively burdensome than a private limited company or limited liability partnership. This makes partnerships an attractive form for many small businesses who want their administration to be as streamlined as possible.

The major drawbacks with ordinary partnerships are that they do not have a separate legal personality and ordinary partners do not have the protection of limited liability. Partners in an ordinary partnership are both jointly and severally liable for the debts of the business. This means that one partner could find him or herself liable for all the debts of the business.

Although ordinary partnerships are not registered at Companies House, partners do need to register that they are in a partnership with HMRC.

1.4 Limited liability partnerships

Limited liability partnerships share some of the same attributes as both ordinary partnerships and limited companies.

Limited liability partnerships were introduced into UK law by the Limited Liability Partnerships Act 2000. Limited liability partnerships must be registered at Companies House. Once registered, the LLP acquires a separate legal personality, and the partners are protected by limited liability. Limited liability partnerships must have "Limited Liability Partnership" or "LLP" at the end of their name.

1 S.1(1) Partnership Act 1890.

LLPs have more accounting and administrative requirements than ordinary partnerships, but they share many of the advantages of the corporate form; for example, they can grant floating charges, which may make it easier to raise capital.

At least two of the members of an LLP must be designated members, meaning they have the responsibility to file certain documents and do administrative tasks.

Like ordinary partnerships, LLPs have the freedom to draft their own partnership agreements and unlike the articles of association in a company, these agreements are not public documents.

One reason for the popularity of LLPs is that they can be formed with two companies as members; unlike with private limited companies, there is no requirement that one of the directors is a natural person.

1.5 Private limited companies

The law relating to the private limited company (Ltd) features strongly in this book as it is expected that it will dominate the BLP content in SQE1 and 2. For the purposes of the SQE we are looking at private companies limited by shares. (There are also private companies limited by guarantee, but these are outside the ambit of the SQE syllabus and will not be considered here.)

Private limited companies are registered at Companies House. They can be set up by one person (unlike partnerships, which require at least two.) Private limited companies must have "Ltd" or "limited" at the end of their name.

Companies, once registered, have a separate legal personality. This brings with it many advantages, but most importantly means that shareholders can have limited liability. These concepts are discussed in more detail in Chapter 2.

It is very common for companies to own controlling shares in other companies, and this is often the case with large businesses that seek to protect against future liability by incorporating groups of companies. A company in which another company holds a majority of the voting rights is called a subsidiary. The other company is called a parent or holding company. It is important to note that in principle each company is separate under the law; however, in some areas of the law, statute may intervene to consider them single entities (for example, in competition law).

The administration of small companies, including incorporation and filing requirements, has become much simpler in recent years, but it is worth noting that administrative requirements are more onerous than in ordinary partnerships and sole traderships.

Companies can be useful vehicles for attracting finance to the business; this can be done either through the issuing of shares (equity finance) or borrowing money (debt finance).

The company is largely run by a director or board of directors who will take most of the decisions. Certain big decisions are reserved for the shareholders, however. It is quite common for the shareholders and directors to be the same people, fulfilling different roles. A company can have just one director, but at least one director must be a human being.

1.6 Public limited companies

The SQE syllabus does include public limited companies, but it specifically does not include those public limited companies that have a public listing on a stock exchange.

There are several differences between private and public companies. The fundamental difference is reflected in the words public and private. Shares in private companies may only be issued or transferred privately and cannot be traded publicly on a stock market. Other differences include:

- Regulation of public limited companies is stricter.
- Public listed companies have PLC at the end of their name; private companies have Ltd.
- Public limited companies must have a minimum of £50,000 share capital.
- Public limited companies must have a qualified company secretary.
- Public limited companies must have two directors (in addition to the company secretary).

Many of the advantages of the PLC relate to the ability to sell shares to the public with a listing on the stock exchange. There are other advantages that may appeal to companies, including having the "snob-value" PLC at the end of the name, which is often deemed more prestigious than Ltd and can suggest (often incorrectly) that the company is a very large concern. Even if the company does not have a listing on the stock exchange it can be easier to transfer shares, for example in order to fulfil the requirement of a deceased shareholder's estate.

1.7 Commercial awareness talking point

When advising on business organisations, it is not enough for a solicitor to simply know the law. Understanding the overall context is equally as important. The nature of the business may mean that its volatility indicates that running the business through a limited liability vehicle may be advisable. Similarly, the enterprise could be inherently low-risk and the client may well prefer to go for an organisation that is simple to run and avoids lots of administration. The risk appetite of the client is an important factor as well as the resources at their disposal. There may often be compelling tax efficiency reasons which may make one business form take priority over another. Taxation is discussed further in Chapters 13 to 16.

Chapter 1 revision points

Advantages and disadvantages of business organisations

Business form	Advantages	Disadvantages
Sole trader	Simplicity, least administration. Informal. Easy to maintain control over the business.	No limited liability. Only one person is in the sole partnership.
Partnership (ordinary)	Reduced administration. Easy to maintain control over the business	No limited liability. Partner can be liable for all debts of the partnership. No separate legal personality.
Limited liability partnership (LLP)	Limited liability. Much of the flexibility of an ordinary partnership. Separate legal personality.	Administrative requirements and accounting requirements.
Private limited company (Ltd)	Limited liability, Separate legal personality.	Administrative requirements, filing requirements and accounting requirements.
Public limited company (PLC)	Limited liability. Separate legal personality. Ability to sell shares to the public.	Administrative requirements, filing requirements and accounting requirements. Significantly enhanced regulatory oversight.

Key features of business organisations

Business form	Limited liability	Separate legal personality	Registered at Companies House	Public filing	Flexibility
Sole trader	No	No	No	No	Yes
Partnership	No	No	No	No	Yes
LLP	Yes	Yes	Yes	Yes	Moderate
Ltd	Yes	Yes	Yes	Yes	Moderate
PLC	Yes	Yes	Yes	Yes	No

PART 2

Private limited companies

2 Formation of the company

2.1 Chapter overview

This chapter covers the legal requirements for the incorporation of a private limited company. It explains the meaning and significance of the dual principles of limited liability and separate legal personality. The chapter continues by looking at the rare occasions where contracts are purportedly formed with a company not yet in existence. The filing requirements of incorporation are discussed, and the chapter concludes with thoughts on the appropriate methods of initial finance.

2.2 Incorporation

The term incorporation means the process through which a business, either new or existing, is formally registered at Companies House as a company. Although there are several different types of company, the SQE and therefore this book, is mainly concerned with the incorporation of private limited companies. (By this we mean private companies limited by shares.)

2.3 Limited liability and separate legal personality

The most significant feature of a private limited company is that, once registered, it acquires a separate legal personality, and this means that the shareholders in the company can take advantage of limited liability. Although the twin features of separate personality and limited liability arise from statute, it is the analysis of these features in the case of *Salomon v A Salomon & Co Ltd*[1] that underlines their importance.

Separate legal personality means that a company is in law an entirely separate being to those who set it up. In fact, it is regarded in law as separate from every person and every other company. Limited liability means that the shareholders' personal liability for the obligations of the company is limited to the nominal value of their fully paid-up shares. The combination of these two principles means that a company, as a separate legal personality, is itself responsible in law for its own obligations. In the event of a dispute, it is the company, rather than the shareholders, who will be sued.

1 [1896] UKHL 1, [1897] AC 22.

DOI: 10.4324/9781003289760-4

This situation is particularly relevant when a company becomes wound up. Although the assets of the company are available for distribution to creditors, the creditors normally have no recourse to the personal assets of the shareholders. Thus, the position of a small company's shareholders can be infinitely preferable to that of partners in an ordinary partnership in the event of a winding up.

Other advantages of separate legal personality are that a company can form contracts and hold property. As the shares in a company are personal property that can be transferred to others or transmitted under a will, a company need not cease to exist on the death or retirement of a shareholder. This advantage is referred to as perpetual succession.

2.4 When separate legal personality does not apply

There have been various occasions where the courts have deemed it appropriate to make an exception to the principle of separate legal personality.

On very rare occasions, the courts still reserve the jurisdiction to intervene and "pierce" the corporate veil if they feel that the corporate form is being abused. Please note, this is a highly contested area and because it is such a complex area, it is not likely to be suited to the format of an SQE1 multiple-choice question. Students do need to be aware that the courts have reserved this jurisdiction, even though it is not very clear when it will apply. One point to note is that examples of "piercing" the veil are very rare, and the courts will not intervene just because the interests of justice suggest they should.

There have been isolated cases in the past where the courts have sought to treat separately incorporated companies in a group as one single economic unit, but this line of cases has been doubted in a number of key decisions[2] and it is clear that, barring a statutory provision to the contrary, each company in a corporate group will have a separate legal personality.

More commonly, other areas of law may intervene; for example, it is possible, although very uncommon, for parent companies to owe tortious duties of care to the employees of subsidiary companies.[3] Similarly, it is possible for companies to hold property on trust for a shareholder.[4]

By far the most common instance where separate legal personality is ignored, is when parliament decrees it so. There are many examples of this in the *Insolvency Act 1986* (as amended) and these will be referred to in Chapter 17.

2 *Woolfson v Strathclyde Regional Council* [1978] UKHL 5; *Adams v Cape* [1990] Ch 433.
3 *Chandler v Cape* [2012] EWCA (Civ) 525.
4 *Prest v Petrodel* UKSC 34, 4 All ER 673.

2.5 Unexpected consequences of separate legal personality

It is important to be aware of the potential consequences of separate legal personality that can bring surprising results. The decision in *Salomon* has had a number of consequences quite apart from the newfound ability of small businesses to incorporate and take advantage of limited liability. Case law demonstrates that companies can hold property and that company property is usually held legally and beneficially by the company itself. (It is possible for a company to act as a trustee over property, but there is a very strong presumption against a company holding property on trust for its shareholders.) Although shareholders are often referred to as residual claimants, being entitled to any surplus when a company is wound up, they do not own the company property until that point. This meant in one case that, despite being both the principal shareholder and creditor of the company, a businessman was unable to claim on an insurance policy in his own name because he lacked an insurable interest in the insured property.[5]

There are also consequences stemming from the ability of a company to contract on its own behalf. The decision in *Lee*[6] revolved around whether the deceased Mr Lee, in his position as shareholder and managing director of a company in which he held all but one of 3,000 shares, was also an employee of the company within the meaning of a New Zealand statute. The Privy Council, largely on the basis that a company is able to form its own contracts by virtue of the Salomon principle, held that Mr Lee was an employee and therefore Mrs Lee was entitled to compensation under the statute. An important point to note on this case is the recognition that Mr Lee was acting in a number of roles regarding the formation of the contract of employment, being the agent (as a director) in arranging it as well as the employee. To a lawyer not versed in company law tradition these cases may appear to be somewhat contrived, not to say absurd. In *Lee* and *Macaura* the companies in question were under the complete control of one shareholder. However, another view is that they are also not only consistent but logical with the Salomon principle, being a direct corollary of the recognition that once registered, a company acquires a separate legal personality. As a direct result of the separate legal personality, a company is able to hold property and to form contracts in its own right; both factors have been hugely beneficial to business. It might be contended therefore that the occasional absurd consequence might be regarded as a price worth paying.

2.6 Pre-incorporation contracts

This area considers the situation where, prior to incorporation, someone forms a contract on behalf of the company. In short, unless that person expressly excludes the

5 *Macaura v Northern Assurance Co Ltd* [1925] AC 619.
6 *Lee v Lee's Air Farming Ltd* [1961] AC 12.

effect of the following section in the *Companies Act 2006* – they will be liable for obligations under the contract.

> s.51(1) A contract that purports to be made by or on behalf of a company at a time when the company has not been formed has effect, subject to any agreement to the contrary, as one made with the person purporting to act for the company or as agent for it, and he is personally liable on the contract accordingly.

2.7 Requirements for registration

The first step of incorporation is to complete form IN01 and submit it together with the memorandum of association and the articles of association (but only if the applicant has opted not to adopt the model articles.)

The memorandum of association is a document that sets out the names of the initial shareholders and is signed by them. The memorandum of association cannot be altered after incorporation.

The articles of association is a document that sets out the constitution of the company. The articles can be amended by the company after incorporation, and any amendment must be communicated to Companies House.

The following information is required on the IN01 Form:

- Company name.
- Registered office.
- First directors.
- Directors' residential and service addresses.
- Company secretary (if there is one).
- Company secretary's service address (if there is one).
- First shareholders' names and addresses details of shareholding
- Statement of capital.
- People of significant control (PSC) – a person (can be a legal person also) who holds more than 25% of the shares, or more than 25% of the voting rights, or holds the right to appoint or remove a majority of the board.
- Statement of compliance.

2.8 Initial financing considerations

In setting up a new company, finance will be a key consideration. Finance is discussed in Chapter 5 in more detail, but one aspect is worth mentioning here. Businesspeople who subscribe to be shareholders in a new company should be aware that the number of their ordinary shares relates directly to their voting power in the company.

2.9 Commercial awareness talking points

The decision to incorporate a private limited company has consequences. The obvious advantages of limited liability are balanced by the statutory requirements for accountability and publicity which start at the point of incorporation. For small companies, the process of incorporation is relatively straightforward and cheap; however, the requirements are ongoing, and businesspeople need to ensure that they comply with the company rules throughout the lifetime of the company.

Decisions about the initial financing of the company are significant also and can have far-reaching consequences in terms of what controls others have over the future direction of the business.

Chapter 2 revision points

- Companies once properly registered at Companies House acquire a separate legal personality (SLP).
- SLP has many advantages, notably enabling shareholders to take advantage of limited liability.
- SLP is usually respected by the courts but there are rare occasions when the corporate veil is pierced. More commonly, other areas of law may intervene and there are many examples where Parliament has decreed that SLP does not apply. Many of these are in the *Insolvency Act 1986* (as amended).
- The process of incorporation requires the filling in of an online form at Companies House together with a memorandum of association and articles of association, unless the model articles are adopted.
- Decisions on the initial financing of the company are important and can affect who controls the company in the future.

3 The constitution of the company

3.1 Chapter overview

To a large extent, the constitution of the company means the articles of association, a document that every company must have from incorporation.

This chapter considers the nature of the articles, their contractual nature, how they can be altered, and how they can be enforced.

The chapter also considers shareholders' agreements, which are very useful documents that can regulate the affairs of shareholders and in many ways can be more flexible than the articles.

3.2 The articles of association

All companies are required to have a set of articles of association on incorporation. Sometimes referred to as the internal rule book of the company, the articles are the constitution of the company and contain rules governing how it is run. The articles are an outward facing public document that is filed at Companies House. Any change to the articles must be filed at Companies House.

When advising on any company matter, it is often necessary for a solicitor to examine the articles of association as this is usually the key document to understand how a company is meant to operate. Many provisions in the *Companies Act 2006* are not mandatory and will only apply if the articles of association are silent in a particular area.

Fundamentally, the articles of association will give a director of a company most of the powers required to run the company, through a general management clause.

3.3 Model articles

Although it is a statutory requirement for companies to have articles, it would be impractical and far too bureaucratic to expect every small business that wished to incorporate to spend time or money drafting bespoke articles. If a company does not choose to use a bespoke set, it will be incorporated with the proscribed model articles. On the SQE1, it is likely that most company questions will involve the model articles.

DOI: 10.4324/9781003289760-5

An important point to remember is that there are different sets of model articles, depending on the type of company. The most common set you will come across in the SQE1 are the model articles for private companies limited by shares. Please note also that the model articles are updated from time to time – if a company chooses to adopt the model articles it will adopt the set that is in place when it is incorporated. If the company wishes to adopt a new set of articles it will have to do so explicitly. There are plenty of companies who still have Table A, the default articles that were in place before the *Companies Act 2006* came into place.

3.4 Model articles with amendments

If a business is happy with most of the model articles but not all, a common practice is to adopt the model articles with amendments.

The amendments needed will obviously vary from company to company according to need. Below are two of the most common amendments made.

- **Model article 14 (1)**

  MA 14(1) dictates that, unless disapplied, a director is prevented from participating in the decision-making process and counting in the quorum where they have a disclosable interest.

  > 14(1) If a proposed decision of the directors is concerned with an actual or proposed transaction or arrangement with the company in which a director is interested, that director is not to be counted as participating in the decision-making process for quorum or voting purposes.

  This provision relates to one of the fiduciary duties of directors referred to later in this book in Chapter 9. Although **MA 14 (3)** enables the shareholders to disapply 14(1) by an ordinary resolution, this is potentially cumbersome in a small company, therefore it is often excluded.
- **Pre-emption rights**

  Pre-emption rights are existing shareholders' rights of first refusal on an issue of new shares by the company. The model articles do not refer to rights of pre-emption, but they are contained in the *Companies Act 2006*. To give the company more flexibility, these rights may be excluded or amended by a provision in the articles. Companies may also choose to include pre-emption rights on share transfers when a shareholder sells shares. Pre-emption rights are discussed in greater detail in Chapter 5.

3.5 The articles as a contract

The words of S.33 *Companies Act 2006* purport to bind the company and the shareholders to the terms of the company's constitution (for all intents and purposes – the articles of association). The section is known as the statutory contract. This provision has given rise to a complex group of cases and an even more complex body of academic literature devoted to the enforceability of this statutory contract.

For the purposes of the SQE, exploration of this academically interesting area is not required, but it is worth noting that although the shareholders and company are bound together by the articles in a contractual way, it is not always possible for a shareholder to sue on this contract. This is particularly the case if the articles attempt to grant a shareholder a right which is not directly linked to a shareholding, such as voting rights. Shareholders' rights in the articles to be the company solicitor or to be a director have been found to be unenforceable.

Despite the above, there are clauses, frequently inserted in the articles of association, that can give shareholders significant protections, for example weighted voting rights that apply in particular circumstances.

3.6 Amending the articles

One unusual feature of the articles as a contract is that they can be amended without the agreement of all the shareholders. This can be achieved by special resolution (a 75% vote) of the shareholders.

In some situations, there can be additional requirements for an alteration of the articles if this affects the rights of different classes of shares.

3.7 Shareholders' agreements

These are commonly used by shareholders starting up a company, either by all the shareholders or some of them. Unlike the articles, these agreements cannot bind the company, and attempts to do so have been held to be unenforceable by the courts. Shareholder agreements are very common and are often a very effective way of protecting shareholders' interest outside the company law machinery. These are contracts that set out how the shareholders want the company to be run. If any shareholders act in breach of the contract, they can be sued for breach of contract. Unlike the articles of association, shareholder agreements are not public documents and are not filed at Companies House.

3.8 Commercial awareness talking points

There are several key take-home points to make about the articles in respect of commercial awareness. Deciding on which set of articles to adopt is a key decision for the company. Below is a non-exhaustive list of considerations:

3.8.1 Are there other shareholders and what proportion of the shares are held by the client?

Company law is essentially based on the principle of majority rule. Usually, anyone with a majority shareholding has the power to exercise most control over the company. If a client is not a majority shareholder and is concerned about losing control or influence in the company, then it may be sensible to try to amend the articles with protections, such as weighted voting rights. Similarly, as many clauses may not be enforceable in the articles, it might be very sensible to duplicate provisions in a shareholders' agreement.

3.8.2 Do the articles restrict share transfers?

Under the model articles, the board has the discretion to refuse to register a share transfer. This power is usually a sensible provision in the articles of a private limited company because it ensures that the company can prevent shares being transferred to people who it does not want to associate with. The power can lead to problems where shareholders fall out and can no longer work together. In these situations, it is not uncommon for a minority shareholder to be left in a company against their will, often unable to get a return on their investments. To prevent situations like this leading to very expensive litigation, it is advisable to cater for a possible later falling out in a shareholders' agreement with an exit clause of some description.

3.8.3 Is it a family-run company?

According to Companies House, about two-thirds of all companies are family-run. It is not the easiest thing to say to a client, but it is sensible to advise on the potential for family breakdowns to impact on relations within the company. The use of shareholders' agreements and sensible provisions in the articles is equally important in the family context as in the business context. An obvious example of this can be seen in the case law relating to weighted voting clauses.

3.8.4 Is Model Article 14 suitable for the company?

MA 14 is discussed above. The decision as to whether to have this in the articles is particularly important where there are a small number of directors, and this may cause problems for companies if the director in question cannot be counted in the forum.

3.8.5 Is there a provision to remove a director?

Although there is a provision in the *Companies Act 2006* that guarantees shareholders the right to remove a director at a general meeting with an ordinary resolution, companies can also have a provision in the articles that requires a director to resign if called upon to do so by the rest of the board.

3.8.6 Does the company need a provision to change its name?

The *Companies Act 2006* stipulates that a change of name requires a special resolution of shareholders unless a provision in the articles gives the board power to make the change.

Chapter 3 revision points

- All companies must adopt a set of articles that are registered at Companies House.
- The articles are the constitution of the company and govern how it is run, within the parameters of the *Companies Act 2006* and the law in general.
- On incorporation, a company can choose to either draft its own articles, adopt the model articles, or adopt the model articles but with amendments.
- The articles form a statutory contract between the shareholders and the company. Please note that shareholders may not be able to enforce rights in the articles that do not relate directly to their shares.
- The articles may be amended by special resolution (75% vote of shareholders).
- Shareholder agreements are contractual agreements entered into by shareholders separate from the company. They can contain clauses about how the shareholders expect the company to be run. Although these cannot bind the company, parties to the contract can sue to enforce the terms.

4 Roles in the company

4.1 Chapter overview

This short chapter is intended to give a brief explanation of the various roles that people can have within the company. It is important to focus on the role itself rather than the individual, because quite often people can occupy different roles at the same time. For example, it is very common for shareholders to also be directors.

4.2 Shareholders/members

In most circumstances the term member and shareholder can be used interchangeably. A shareholder is someone who has been issued shares in the company and a member is a shareholder whose shareholding is registered on the register of members.

Ownership of shares gives the shareholder various rights in the company which are determined by the articles of association and the general law.

Shareholders are not responsible for the day-to-day management of the company, but they are required to take certain big decisions.

Shareholders can make money from the company through being paid dividends on their shares or by transferring their shares.

4.3 Different types of shareholder

The various types of shares that can be issued are discussed later in Chapter 5. It is worth noting at this stage that the role of a shareholder will depend on the type of share that they hold, and the rights attached to those shares detailed in the articles of association. For example, preference shareholders may well have additional rights when it comes to the distribution of dividends, but they often will not have the same voting rights as ordinary shareholders.

DOI: 10.4324/9781003289760-6

4.4 Directors

All sets of articles should contain a clause giving directors the power to run the company. This is often referred to as the general management clause. This means that directors can take most of the decisions on behalf of the company. Certain very important decisions are reserved for shareholders.

Every private limited company must have at least one human director who is at least 16.

Because directors have wide powers over the company, the law imposes many duties and responsibilities on them, to control the exercise of their discretion.

Who appoints the director will depend on the articles of association. If the articles are silent then the powers rests with the shareholders. Under the model articles, appointment can be by the board or by the shareholders.

Shareholders have a statutory right[1] to remove a director with an ordinary resolution at a general meeting. (Note that this cannot be achieved with a written resolution.) Special notice of 28 days is required before a meeting in which the resolution is to be voted on.

4.5 *De facto* and shadow directors

The definition of a director within the *Companies Act 2006* states:

> In the Companies Acts "director" includes any person occupying the position of director, by whatever name called.[2]

This definition is quite broad and means that it is possible to be a *de facto* director (a director in fact) even if there has been no formal appointment process. Someone can be considered a *de facto* director if they have been held out as such, but this is not essential, and the courts have adopted a nuanced approach based on the individual facts of the situation. *De facto* directors owe fiduciary duties to the company in the same way as formally appointed directors.

The *Companies Act 2006* also contains a definition for a shadow director:

> In the Companies Acts "shadow director", in relation to a company, means a person in accordance with whose directions or instructions the directors of the company are accustomed to act.[3]

1 S.168 *Companies Act 2006*.
2 S.250 *Companies Act 2006*.
3 S.251(1) *Companies Act 2006*.

The distinction between *de facto* and shadow directors is really one of visibility. The *de facto* director openly assumes the role of director, but without formal appointment. A shadow director, as the name suggests, remains hidden in the background and exerts their influence unseen by others outside the company.

4.6 Company secretaries

Private limited companies are not required to have a company secretary, but many do. The functions of the company secretary are not defined in statute but usually involve critical aspects of the internal and external running of the company, such as arranging meetings, maintaining the company books, and filing documents with Companies House.

4.7 Auditors

Unless exempt, a company is required to have its annual accounts audited every year. There are exemptions for small companies that apply to a large proportion of the businesses of the UK. Even if a small company is exempt, shareholders holding 10% of the shares can require the company to request an audit.

Auditors are usually appointed by an ordinary resolution of shareholders, but the board also has the power to appoint and may appoint the auditor in the first accounting year.

Auditors can only be removed before the expiry of their term by ordinary resolution of shareholders at a general meeting. Special notice of 28 days is required before a meeting in which the resolution is to be voted on.

4.8 Other stakeholders in the company

At this point it is worth commenting on other parties who are closely affected by the activities of the company. These are sometimes referred to as stakeholders in the company such as employees, suppliers, trade creditors, and customers. Modern corporate law does consider these stakeholders at various points and this book will focus on them again in Chapters 8 and 17.

4.9 Commercial awareness talking points

Focusing on roles as opposed to individuals is important for businesspeople, particularly if they are occupying multiple positions. The obvious example of this is a shareholder who is also a director of a company because directors owe quite stringent fiduciary duties to the company that they must consider when exercising their discretion.

Chapter 4 revision points

- Shareholders are investors in companies and hold shares.
- Shares can be issued under different terms; this means that the rights of shareholders can differ.
- Directors are empowered to run the company by the articles of association.
- Rules on appointment of directors will depend on the articles of association.

5 Financing the company

5.1 Chapter overview

Corporate finance is a large subject that becomes very complex quite quickly. There are core aspects that are usually delivered in company law modules on LLB courses. The SQE1 curriculum details the following areas:

- Funding options: debt and equity.
- Types of security.
- Distribution of profits and gains.
- Financial records, information, and accounting requirements.

The first three will be discussed in this chapter; financial records, information, and accounting requirements will be discussed in Chapter 13.

5.2 Equity and debt finance

Businesses need to decide how to finance the company. It will either be by equity or debt financing, or a mixture of the two. It is clearly a requirement to understand basic differences between these two forms. Put simply, when references are made to equity finance this usually means shares in a company. Debt finance usually means loans to a company from a financial institution.

5.3 The nature of shares

Shares are personal property and things in action. This means that they contain rights that can potentially be enforced by a court. The extent of the rights attached to each share will depend on the articles of association. A company can have different classes of shares with different rights.

5.4 Ordinary shares

Most shares issued by companies are ordinary shares and it is very common for companies to only have ordinary shares. Ordinary shares usually carry voting rights

DOI: 10.4324/9781003289760-7

and entitle the shareholder to participate in excess assets, if there are any, in a winding-up. It is not uncommon for companies to have more than one class of ordinary shares with differing rights attached (often referred to as A shares, B shares and so on).

5.5 Preference shares

Preference shares are shares that simply enjoy some preference over ordinary shares, often entitling the holder to higher dividends or a preferential right to participate in a winding-up ahead of ordinary shareholders. Preferential shares do not normally have voting rights.

The purpose of a company issuing preference shareholders is to bring in additional money into the company as, in exchange for preferential treatment, they will be more expensive to purchase.

5.6 Share dividends

People who have invested in a company can get a return on their investment either by selling their shares for a profit or by receiving dividend payments.

A company can only make a dividend payment out of accumulated, realised profit.

Under the model articles, an ordinary resolution of shareholders is required to declare a dividend.

Share dividends are treated differently to other forms of income for tax purposes. This can mean that it is advantageous for a director of a company who holds shares to receive dividends instead of a salary. For example, in the 2022/2023 tax year, shareholders have a dividend allowance of £2,000 meaning that they can be paid £2,000 in dividends without paying tax, irrespective of what band of income tax they are in. The taxation of dividend income is examined in Chapter 14.

5.7 Allotting and issuing shares

The expressions "allotting" and "issuing" are often used interchangeably although they have subtly different meanings. When shares are allotted, the person to whom the shares are allotted has the right to be included in the register of members. Shares are issued at the point when the person to whom the shares have been allotted is placed on the register of members.

The rules on the allotment of shares depend upon the type of company and also the number of classes of share that a company has.

5.8 Allotting shares in private companies with only one class of share

Providing there is nothing in the articles forbidding it, the board of directors of a private company with only one class of shares has the power to allot shares of the same class.

As most companies in the UK are private companies with only one class of share, it follows that most boards will have this power. The power can be excluded by the articles, but it is not excluded by the model articles.

5.9 Allotting shares in private companies with more than one class of share

Directors in companies with more than one class of share can allot shares providing they either have the authority from the articles of association or they are authorised by a company resolution. This can be authorised by an ordinary resolution.

5.10 Pre-emption rights

The *Companies Act 2006* gives existing shareholders rights of pre-emption. This means that if new shares are issued, existing shareholders must be offered a portion of the new shares proportionate to their existing shareholding. Pre-emption rights are important because they can enable a shareholder to maintain the same level of control of the company.

Pre-emption rights can be excluded by the articles in private limited companies although the model articles do not do this. Pre-emption rights can also be disapplied in a private limited company. Both exclusion and disapplication of pre-emption rights require a special resolution of shareholders.

5.11 Transferring shares

In a private limited company shares are freely transferable subject to any restrictions in the articles. It is very common for directors to have the discretion to refuse to register a share transfer. The model articles contain a provision giving directors the power to refuse to register share transfers.

5.12 Share buybacks

Although there are restrictions on companies buying their own shares, this is permitted in some circumstances and can be very useful as it can mean that the company is able to buy the shares of a shareholder who is no longer happy in the company. A buyback can be very useful for all concerned because it is often very difficult for a shareholder to transfer shares in a private limited company where there is no readily available market for the shares. A share buyback is only possible if the articles do not prohibit it.

If the shares are bought out of a company's distributable profits, the shareholders may approve the buyback by ordinary resolution.

If the shares (or some of the shares) are bought out of a company's capital, the process is much more complex. There are various filing and publicity requirements, and the directors must make a solvency statement with an auditor's report annexed to it. In addition to the ordinary resolution to authorise the buyback, the shareholders must approve the use of capital by special resolution. The company must place a notice in the *London Gazette* and either place a notice in a national newspaper or notify every creditor in writing about the special resolution. Creditors are able to apply to court to object to the buyback within five weeks.

5.13 Types of debt capital

Debt capital can be divided into two categories. First, and most significant for the SQE and this book, companies often borrow money in the form of loans; this could be through bank loans, overdrafts, and even large-scale syndicated loans. Often, to persuade a lender to lend the required sums, a company may grant the lender a security, a fixed or floating charge, or a director or shareholder may need to offer a personal guarantee.

It is also possible for companies to access the capital markets through the issuing of debt securities – often in the form of bonds. The issuing of bond securities is a much more sophisticated method of raising debt capital and a detailed understanding is beyond the scope of the SQE syllabus.

5.14 Fixed and floating charges

The benefit to a lender having a charge over a borrower's property is that in the event of an insolvency the lender will have some protection as they will be paid before many of the other creditors.

Fixed charges can be granted over particular items of property, often buildings or machinery.

Floating charges can be granted over the whole undertaking, and these can be very useful for a company as the existence of a floating charge does not prevent the company trading with the assets in the normal course of business. Floating charges rank behind fixed charges in a distribution (when a company is wound up), so a lender will usually prefer a fixed charge if they can have one.

Fixed and floating charges need to be registered at Companies House and fixed charges on land also need to be registered with the Land Registry.

5.15 Personal guarantees

An alternative way of providing security to a lender is for a shareholder or director to offer a personal guarantee. This is often a requirement of a lender if a company has a short trading history and no assets that a charge can be granted over. Although personal guarantees are useful in setting up companies, they do negate the advantages that are offered by limited liability as the lender will be able to sue the shareholder director if the company fails to repay the loan.

5.16 Commercial awareness talking points

Corporate finance is a very complex topic, and a day-one solicitor is not expected to have a comprehensive knowledge of all aspects. The key takeaway point, however, is to understand the fundamental differences between equity and debt finance. Some of these are summarised in the table below.

	Equity	Debt
Meaning	Shares	Loans
Return on investment	Dividends	Repayment and interest
Regularity of Returns	Irregular – dividend payments can only be made from profits	Regular payments – usually monthly
Tax treatment	Not tax deductible	Interest payments are potentially tax deductible as a business expense
Control over the company	Ordinary shares come with certain rights that include the right to vote and take part in major company decision-making	A loan is an arm's length contractual arrangement which usually means that the lender will have no control over the running of the company provided the loan payments are made
Availability	To encourage shareholders to invest large amounts of money in a newly formed company may be tricky as the company has no track record	With newly formed companies it can often be difficult to raise money in loans as the company will have no credit history Directors of newly formed companies often have to offer personal guarantees to the lender

	Investors could be incentivised by issuing them with preference shares – these typically will have rights to a higher dividend	For more established companies with assets this can be a lot easier because the company will be able to grant a fixed or floating charge to the lender. This should mean that it is also cheaper to borrow the money as the interest rate offered may be lower

Chapter 5 revision points

- Companies require finance to develop business projects.
- The two types of finance are equity (shares) and debt (loans).
- Issuing shares in a company may affect controlling interests in the company.
- Shares can be issued with different rights relating to voting or payment of dividends.
- Shareholders have rights in the company that are set out in the articles of association.
- Companies can grant floating and fixed charges that provide security for lenders and may mean that the company gets a more favourable loan deal or is able to borrow more.

6 Shareholders' decision-making

6.1 Chapter overview

Shareholders are not responsible for the day-to-day running of the company. This means that most decisions in a company are taken by directors under their powers of general management in the articles of association.

Directors are often shareholders too. Sometimes in very small companies it can be confusing for a businessperson to know in what capacity they are acting.

Broadly speaking, the board of directors will make most decisions, but certain important decisions will be reserved for shareholders.

Some decisions must be made by shareholders because of the *Companies Act 2006*, others because they are stipulated in the company's articles.

6.2 Ordinary resolutions

If an ordinary resolution of the shareholders is required, this means a bare majority of the votes cast at a general meeting or 50% +1 of the votes. Note, most resolutions can also be passed by written resolution.

Where a private limited company has adopted the model articles, these procedures require an ordinary resolution:

- To remove a director.
- To authorise a substantial property transaction.
- To authorise a loan to a director.
- To authorise a payment for loss of office.
- To authorise a share buyback.
- To remove an auditor.
- To ratify a director's breach of duty.

DOI: 10.4324/9781003289760-8

6.3 Special resolutions

If a special resolution is required, this means a 75% majority, that is, three-quarters of the votes cast at a general meeting. Note that most resolutions can also be passed by written resolution.

Where a private limited company has adopted the model articles, the following require special resolutions:

- To change the name of the company.
- To amend the articles of association.
- To disapply pre-emption rights.
- To approve a payment out of capital.

6.4 General meetings

Formal meetings of shareholders are called general meetings. There is no longer a statutory requirement for private companies to have an annual general meeting (AGM). There may however be a provision of the articles that stipulates one, and a general meeting can be necessary in some circumstances (for example, the removal of a director or removal of an auditor.) There is no requirement for an AGM in the model articles.

- **Calling**

  General meetings are called by the board. The board may also be required to call general meetings by shareholders holding at least 5% of the issued voting shares.
- **Notice**

  Unless a longer period is stipulated in the articles, the notice period for a general meeting of a private company is a minimum of 14 clear days. This means that the day of notice and the day of the meeting are not included in the calculation. Hence, if notice is given on the second day of the month, the earliest that the meeting can take place is the seventeenth.

  A general meeting may be called on short notice with the consent of a majority of the company's shareholders providing they also hold 90% or more of the voting shares.

  Some resolutions require special notice of 28 days, such as the removal of a director or an auditor.

  Where a board of directors has been instructed to call a general meeting by the shareholders, the meeting must be called within 21 days of them being instructed for a date in no more than 28 days' time.
- **Quorum**

  Where there is only one shareholder in the company, the quorum requirement is one. In all other circumstances, unless stipulated differently in the articles, the quorum requirement for a general meeting is two.

- **Voting**

  Under the model articles, unless a poll vote is requested, voting is on a show of hands and each shareholder has one vote.

  In a poll vote, votes are counted according to the number of voting shares held. Under the model articles, poll votes may be demanded by the following:

  The chairman of the meeting.

  The directors.

  Two or more persons having the right to vote on the resolution.

  A person or persons representing not less than one-tenth of the total voting rights of all the shareholders having the right to vote on the resolution.

6.5 Written resolutions

One of the important developments in the modern company has been the use of written resolutions in private limited companies. (Written resolutions are not permitted in public companies.) Although these have been used for many years, their use is now detailed in statute.

Written resolutions can be proposed by the board and by shareholders who control 5% of the voting shares.

In all but two instances, companies can use the written resolution procedure. This can be very useful and more efficient as it negates the need for a general meeting. The two instances where it is not possible are where an ordinary resolution is put forward to remove a director or an auditor (in both circumstances there is a right to protest removal that can only be exercised at a general meeting).

The written resolutions are circulated and are open for response for 28 days; however, the resolution is passed once the required majority (50% +1 vote or 75%) of shareholders entitled to vote is reached.

6.6 Minutes

Minutes must be taken of all general meetings and stored for ten years. A record must also be made of any written ordinary or special resolutions.

6.7 Commercial awareness talking point

The role of the shareholder is not the day-to-day management of the company. Nevertheless, the biggest decisions are usually left to the shareholders, either because the *Companies Act 2006* makes this so, or because the company is organised that way. The principle of majority rule runs throughout company law and most decisions require an ordinary resolution. It is probably worth memorising those decisions that require a special resolution.

Most of the time, numbers of votes will equate to the number of shares that a shareholder holds. Sometimes, however, shareholders may hold shares that do not have voting rights. Conversely, there can be instances where a shareholder may have weighted voting rights. All such rights will be stipulated in the articles of association which mean that the careful study of this document is vital when advising a company law client.

Chapter 6 revision points

- Certain important decisions are reserved for the shareholders.
- These decisions are taken as resolutions, either ordinary or special.
- Ordinary resolutions require a bare majority of votes.
- Special resolutions require 75% of votes.
- Resolutions can be made in general meetings.
- All resolutions can be passed using the written procedure with the exception of resolutions to remove a director or an auditor.
- There are various rules relating to calling a meeting, notice periods, voting, and quorum.

7 Directors' decision-making

7.1 Chapter overview

The board of directors are the primary decision-making body in the company. They will make nearly all the decisions of the company. This can happen in a regular board meeting or by resolutions outside of meetings.

7.2 Board resolutions

Under the model articles, resolutions at a board meeting are passed on a majority. Board resolutions do not have to be made at a board meeting, provided the board are in unanimous agreement.

7.3 Board meetings

- **Calling**
  Any director may call a board meeting. Unless it is stated otherwise in the articles, directors must be given reasonable notice of the meeting. The meaning of "reasonable" will relate to the surrounding circumstances. It may be reasonable to call a meeting at short notice in a crisis.
- **Quorum**
  The rules for the quorum are set out in the articles. In the model articles the quorum is set at two. Note that there are further clauses in the model articles which mean that a private company with just one director can operate also. The model articles state that a director with an interest in a transaction cannot vote or be counted in the quorum on that issue. If necessary, this clause can be disapplied by ordinary resolution of shareholders.
- **Chair**
  Under the model articles, the board may appoint one of the directors as chair. If present, the nominated person will also chair general meetings.
- **Voting**
  Under the model articles, board resolutions in meetings are passed by a majority. In the event of a tie, the chair of the board has a casting vote.

DOI: 10.4324/9781003289760-9

In certain circumstances, a director may be precluded from voting or being counted in the quorum on a particular issue because of a conflict of interest (discussed in more detail in Chapter 8.)

- **Minutes**

  Minutes of meetings must be taken and stored for ten years after the meeting. The model articles also require records of resolutions taken outside board meetings to be stored for ten years.

7.4 Commercial awareness talking point

Much of the law relating to the process of directors' decision-making reflects commercial reality. There has been a conscious effort of the legislature to ensure that the decision-making process is as streamlined as possible. Certainly, the ability of boards to meet virtually has been a great benefit during the Covid-19 pandemic. The fact that the law also takes a realistic view for resolutions where there is unanimous agreement is also laudable. Businesses do need to be aware of the requirements of record-keeping and minute-taking, particularly as memories of corporate events often differ when businesspeople fall out with each other later.

Chapter 7 revision points

- Most decisions of the company are made by directors.
- If resolutions are unanimous, they can be made outside of a board meeting.
- There are various rules relating to calling, voting, notice, and quorum.
- Minutes must be taken of board meetings and retained for ten years.

8 Directors' duties

8.1 Chapter overview

In a similar way to trustees and their beneficiaries, directors owe certain duties to their companies. The following duties are codified as general duties in the *Companies Act 2006*:

- Duty to act within powers.
- Duty to promote the success of the company.
- Duty to exercise independent judgment.
- Duty to exercise reasonable care, skill, and diligence.
- Duty to avoid conflicts of interest.
- Duty not to accept benefits from third parties.
- Duty to declare interest in proposed transaction or arrangement.
- Duty to declare interest in existing transaction or arrangement.

Each duty is considered in turn and consideration is given to how these duties can be enforced.

8.2 To whom are the duties owed?

The duties are owed to the company itself as a separate legal personality and not to individual shareholders. This has major implications for enforcement as the company itself is the person who can most easily bring an action for breach of duty (at least in times of solvency). Chapter 10 discusses the exceptional situations where a shareholder can bring an action for breach.

8.3 Duty to act within powers

This is two duties in one:

- The duty to act in accordance with the constitution.
- The duty to only exercise powers for the purposes for which they are conferred.

The duty to act in accordance with the constitution means that directors must follow the rules laid out in the articles of association.

DOI: 10.4324/9781003289760-10

It is common for bespoke articles to contain a clause that directors need authorisation from either the board or shareholders before entering a contract for over a set amount. Note that if a director were in breach, the contract would probably still be enforceable by the third party, but the director could be sued for breach by the company.

The duty to only exercise powers for the purposes for which they are conferred is sometimes referred to as the proper purpose doctrine. A breach may occur if a director exercises a power for a substantially different purpose than the proper purpose for which the power was given.

Much of the case law in this area relates to directors issuing shares for the purpose of manipulating voting rights within a company. The main purpose of issuing shares in a company is to raise capital – manipulating voting rights could be a substantially different purpose.

Liability for breach does not depend on bad faith or dishonesty. The director can still be in breach if he or she is seeking to promote the success of the company.

8.4 Duty to promote the success of the company

The duty to promote the success of the company (S.172 *Companies Act 2006*) is a central duty of directors and reference is made to this duty in several areas of the Companies Act, notably in the derivative action which will be discussed in Chapter 10. Although in the SQE sections of statutes will not feature a great deal, it is possible that S.172 *Companies Act 2006* could be expressly stated in an SQE1 question as the duty features in various areas of Business Law and Practice.

What a director must do under this duty is act honestly and in good faith to promote the success of the company for the benefit of the shareholders as a whole. This is very much a subjective test – it is what the individual director honestly believes promotes the success of the company.

Under S.172, directors are also required to have regard to other matters, including those in the list below:

(a) the likely consequences of any decision in the long term,
(b) the interests of the company's employees,
(c) the need to foster the company's business relationships with suppliers, customers and others,
(d) the impact of the company's operations on the community and the environment,
(e) the desirability of the company maintaining a reputation for high standards of business conduct, and
(f) the need to act fairly as between members of the company.

8.5 Duty to exercise independent judgement

Directors have a duty to exercise their own independent judgement when they are making decisions.

There is no breach if the company has previously entered into a valid agreement to restrict future discretion or if the director is acting according to a provision in the articles.

The text of S.173 is set out below:

(1) A director of a company must exercise independent judgment.
(2) This duty is not infringed by his acting –
  (a) in accordance with an agreement duly entered into by the company that restricts the future exercise of discretion by its directors, or
  (b) in a way authorised by the company's constitution.

One circumstance where this duty is likely to be engaged is when a director has been nominated by a shareholder. The director must continue to exercise his own independent judgement as he owes his duties to the company, not the shareholder.

8.6 Duty to exercise reasonable care, skill, and diligence

This duty differs relates to matters of competence as opposed to honesty and loyalty. The duty has many similarities to duties of care owed in common law negligence and duties of care and skill owed by trustees to their beneficiaries. The duty has evolved over time, reflecting the professional development and modern expectations of directors.

The test for the standard of care expected under s.174 *Companies Act 2006* has objective and subjective characteristics as identified in the diagram below.

S.174	Objective	Subjective
A director of a company must exercise reasonable care, skill, and diligence.	Yes	Yes
This means the care, skill, and diligence that would be exercised by a reasonably diligent person with –	Yes	No
the general knowledge, skill, and experience that may reasonably be expected of a person carrying out the functions carried out by the director in relation to the company, and	Yes	Yes
the general knowledge, skill, and experience that the director has.	No	Yes

One way of thinking about this is to consider that there is an expectation on all directors that they will have a basic standard of competence ("a reasonably diligent person") but this can rise depending on the particular role played in the company by that director ("the general knowledge, skill and experience that may reasonably be expected of a person") and also any particular skills and experience that the director actually has ("the general knowledge, skill and experience that the director has.")

For example, if a director had a particular responsibility for one aspect within the company, for example financial management, and he was also professionally qualified as an accountant, it is likely that he would be held to a higher standard of care.

The same test is also applied for wrongful trading in the context of insolvency – this is also within the SQE curriculum and is discussed in Chapter 17.

8.7 Duty to avoid conflicts

Directors have a duty to avoid situations where their own interests conflict with their duties. This is a particularly onerous duty that can appear very harsh in its application. Note that it does not depend in any way on dishonesty, and it can still apply even if the director is acting in the best interests of the company.

The duty often arises in situations where a director takes up a personal opportunity that comes his way during his directorship. Unless there is no reasonable possibility of conflict, the director cannot take up the opportunity without authorisation from the board. The board can only authorise the conflict if it is not prohibited from doing so by the articles. Authorisation can only be made if the conflicted director does not vote and is not counted in the quorum.

If the director makes money out of a corporate opportunity, he will be liable to account for any profits he has made – even if the company has made no loss.

The director can be liable even if the company was unable to take up the opportunity or has previously refused it.

The courts have traditionally applied this duty very strictly and this may appear harsh. It is important to note that full disclosure of potential conflicts and authorisation can completely absolve the director of any blame.

8.8 Duty not to accept benefits from third parties

This is essentially a prohibition against taking bribes. This is in addition to the *Bribery Act 2010* criminal offences that are beyond the scope of SQE.

8.9 Duty to disclose interests in proposed transactions or arrangements

This is very similar to the duty to avoid conflicts considered above. The duty relates to actual or potential conflicts of interest relating to proposed transactions or arrangements with the company.

Subject to the exceptions below, the director must disclose the nature and extent of the interest before the company enters the transaction or arrangement:

- If the director is not aware of the interest, or of the transaction or arrangement in question. Note that the section adds: "For this purpose a director is treated as being aware of matters of which he ought reasonably to be aware."[1]
- If the interest cannot be reasonably regarded as a conflict.
- If the other directors are already aware, or it would be unreasonable for them not to be aware.
- If the interest concerns the director's service contract.

The way notice must be given under this section seems to be quite flexible; it does not have to be at a board meeting.

It is worth noting that even if a director makes a disclosure as required under this section, under the model articles (MA14 (1)), they will not be able to vote on the transaction or arrangement unless MA14(1) is disapplied with an ordinary resolution (MA14(3)).

8.10 Duty to disclose interest in existing transaction or arrangement

This is very similar to the previous duty but comes into effect once the transaction or arrangement has been entered into by the company. This could happen if the director is new to the board, for example. The same exceptions apply:

- If the director is not aware of the interest or the transaction or arrangement. As with the previous duty, the section adds the following: "For this purpose, a director is treated as being aware of matters of which he ought reasonably to be aware."[2]
- If the interest cannot be reasonably regarded as a conflict.
- If the other directors are already aware, or it would be unreasonable for them not to be aware.
- If the interest concerns a director's service contract.

Notice under this section must be given at a board meeting.

1 *S.177(5) Companies Act 2006.*
2 S.182(5) *Companies Act 2006.*

8.11 Ratification of breach of duty

There are provisions in the *Companies Act 2006* which enable a company to ratify (meaning sanction) the breach of duty and effectively adopt whatever the relevant action was.

Ratification requires an ordinary resolution of the shareholders, not including the director in question or any connected persons.

A successful ratification can be very useful to the director as it makes it much harder for a disgruntled shareholder to bring an action.

Some breaches of duty are not capable of ratification and the case law indicates that such cases will often relate to dishonest or oppressive behaviour.

8.12 Court relief for breach of duty

In limited circumstances, if a court finds that a director has acted honestly and reasonably, it may grant relief to a director even if they are in breach of duty under S.1157 *Companies Act 2006*. Rather counterintuitively this can mean that a director could be in breach of the duty to exercise reasonable care, skill, and diligence but may still be found to have acted reasonably within the meaning of S.1157.

8.13 Commercial awareness talking points

The imposition of directors' duties is an inevitable consequence of the powerful position directors are in with the company. Directors, after all, exercise all of the powers of the company through the General Management clause in the articles; therefore duties are imposed by law to control the exercise of this discretion.

It is worth noting, however, that although in some cases the duties can appear harsh, particularly in the case of the conflict duties, provisions are in place to enable directors to avoid sanction providing they are open and honest about their other commitments that may conflict with their duties to the company. This point is important in a wider commercial context because it enables directors to continue to create and take up wider entrepreneurial activities that may well benefit the wider economy as well as themselves.

Although the duty of care, skill, and diligence is much more significant in modern times, the duty is very much designed not to stop directors being entrepreneurial, but it is focused on due diligence. This should mean that directors can be adventurous providing they have adopted an appropriate decision-making process.

When it was first introduced, the duty to promote the success of the company prompted much speculation that it would encourage litigation because it appears to widen the scope of what the director must consider. This has not proven to be the case, but it has become common for companies to have standing items in meeting agendum relating to the duty either explicitly or implicitly.

Chapter 8 revision notes

- Directors owe a range of duties to the company.
- These duties are like those owed by trustees to their beneficiaries.
- There are a range of fiduciary duties and a duty of care, skill, and diligence.
- The fiduciary obligations relating to conflicts are absolute, and directors need to take great care to disclose interests that may potentially conflict.
- Directors may need to seek authorisation from the board if they are to take up opportunities that may conflict with their duties.
- Some breaches of duty are capable of ratification by the shareholders.

9 Transactions with directors requiring shareholder approval

9.1 Chapter overview

In addition to the various conflicts duties and duties to declare interests, the *Companies Act 2006* also contains further provisions to protect the company by requiring shareholder approval for certain transactions with directors. These are substantial property transactions, loans to directors, directors' service contracts, and payments for loss of office.

9.2 Substantial property transactions

Substantial property transactions occur when the company buys or sells a non-cash asset of substantial value from or to a director or a connected person.

Substantial property transactions need shareholder approval by ordinary resolution.

9.2.1 Non-cash assets of substantial value

A non-cash asset is defined in the *Companies Act 2006* as: "Any property or interest in property other than cash."[1] Substantial value means either:

- Property valued at over £100,000 or;
- Property valued at over £5000 that is also valued at over 10% of the company's net asset value.

9.2.2 Connected persons

Connected persons include the director's family. "Family" in this context is defined as:

(a) the director's spouse or civil partner
(b) any other person (whether of a different sex or the same sex) with whom the director lives as partner in an enduring family relationship
(c) the director's children or step-children

1 S.1163 *Companies Act 2006*.

DOI: 10.4324/9781003289760-11

(d) any children or step-children of a person within paragraph (b) (and who are not children or step-children of the director) who live with the director and have not attained the age of 18
(e) the director's parents.[2]

Other companies can also be connected persons where a director or connected person holds at least 20% of the shares or controls at least 20% of the votes at a general meeting.

9.2.3 Effects of breach

Without approval, a substantial property transaction is voidable. Directors of the company and connected persons can be ordered to account to the company and indemnify the company against losses.

9.3 Long-term service contracts

Directors' service contracts with a guaranteed term longer than two years must be approved by the shareholders with an ordinary resolution.

A guaranteed term means the term during which the contract cannot be terminated by the company or can only be terminated in particular circumstances.

Where the contract is terminable on notice by the company, the guaranteed term is the notice period.

Approval is also required where the director is the director of a holding company within the group consisting of that company and its subsidiaries.

A memorandum setting out details of the service contract must be made available to the shareholders in the following ways:

- If a written resolution, it must be sent or submitted to shareholders at or before the time at which the proposed resolution is sent or submitted.
- For resolutions at a meeting, it must be made available for inspection by members of the company at the registered office 15 days prior to the meeting and at the meeting itself.

9.3.1 Civil consequences of breach

If a service contract is agreed without shareholder approval in contravention of the above rules, the contract will be void to the extent that it contravenes the rules. The relevant director's contract will be terminable on reasonable notice.

2 S.253 *Companies Act 2006*.

9.4 Loans to directors

There can be a number of reasons why it will be useful for a director to take a loan from the company; this is often advantageous from a tax perspective. In most instances, the loan will need to be approved by the shareholders with an ordinary resolution.

Prior to passing the ordinary resolution a memorandum setting out the following needs to be made available to the shareholders. The memorandum must specify:

- The nature of the transaction.
- The amount of the loan and its purpose together.
- The extent of the company's liability under any associated transaction.

In the case of a general meeting, the memorandum must be available for inspection 15 days prior to the meeting and at the meeting itself. In the case of a written resolution, it must be circulated at the same time as the resolution.

The following exceptions apply:

- Loans that do not exceed £10,000 when combined with any related transaction do not need to be approved by the shareholders.
- Approval is not required for loans up to £50,000 to provide a director of the company or of its holding company, or a person connected with any such director, with funds to meet expenditure incurred for the purposes of the company, or for the purpose of enabling the director to properly perform duties to the company.[3]

9.5 Payments for loss of office

Payments for loss of office need to be approved by ordinary resolution if they are over £200 and they are not payments that the company is already legally obliged to make.

If a company buys a director's shares for a higher value than would have been paid in ordinary circumstances, the additional sum paid would be considered as a payment for loss of office.

Prior to the passing of the resolution approving the payment, a memorandum must be made available setting out particulars of the proposed payment including its amount.

In the case of a general meeting, the memorandum must be available for inspection 15 days prior to the meeting and at the meeting itself. In the case of a written resolution, it must be circulated at the same time as the resolution.

3 S.204 *Companies Act 2006*.

9.6 Commercial awareness talking point

The point of all of these provisions is to bring added protection for shareholders against potential abuse by directors. The picture here is really about accountability and openness rather than bringing in regulation to stymie creativity. There can be very good reasons for long-term directors' contracts, substantial property transactions, loans to directors, and payments for loss of office – all the law is doing is making sure that these key areas are explicitly brought to the attention of shareholders.

Chapter 9 revision points

- Shareholder approval by ordinary resolution is required for:
- Substantial property transactions and long-term directors' contracts.
- Shareholder approval by ordinary resolution is often needed for:
- Payments to directors for loss of office and loans to directors.
- These provisions are in addition to any of the requirements that directors have to disclose interests to the board.

10 Minority shareholder protection

10.1 Chapter overview

Companies operate on the basis that they are controlled by the majority. Usually, the more shares someone has, the more control they have in the company. Because of the potential for abuse, some remedies are available to minority shareholders. The two main remedies are the unfair prejudice petition and the derivative action. There is also a further remedy called the just and equitable winding-up, a drastic remedy that results in the death of the company.

Because litigation within companies is frequently ruinously expensive and economically deleterious, solicitors often play an important role in suggesting contractual mechanisms that anticipate problems later on in the company's life. This chapter also includes contractual, self-help remedies that can be included in shareholder agreements and the articles of association that can sometimes obviate the need for expensive litigation.

10.2 Unfair prejudice

A shareholder can bring an unfair prejudice petition "if the affairs of the company have been conducted in a manner unfairly prejudicial to the interests of members or a group of shareholders of which the shareholder is a part."[1]

The phrases "affairs of the company" and "interests of members" are interpreted broadly by the courts. Anything that involves a resolution of the company at board or general meeting could be affairs of the company. Interests of members is not restricted to rights in shares; this could include a member's interest in management or even as a creditor of the company.

1 S.994(1)(a) *Companies Act 2006*.

DOI: 10.4324/9781003289760-12

The case law indicates that this will be objectively assessed, and unfair prejudice will normally only arise in the following two instances:

- A breach of the terms under which it was agreed the company would be run.
- Some use of the rules in a manner which equity would regard as contrary to good faith.[2]

10.3 Unfair prejudice and quasi partnerships

The case law indicates that unfair prejudice petitions are more likely to be successful in quasi partnership companies. These are companies that usually have one or more of the following characteristics:

- Associations formed based on mutual confidence.
- Agreements that members would be involved in the running of the company.
- Restrictions on the transfer of shares.[3]

10.4 Examples of unfair prejudicial behaviour

The statutory provisions do not set out the detailed circumstances in which unfair prejudicial conduct can apply. From looking at the case law the following examples can be seen; please note, this is far from comprehensive:

- Exclusion from management.
- Non-payment of dividends.
- Breach of duty.
- Alteration of the constitution.
- Refusal to permit a share transfer.
- Behaviour in breach of a shareholder's agreement.

10.5 Effect of a reasonable offer to buy out shareholder

If a petitioner has been made a reasonable offer by the company, or other shareholders to buy the petitioner's shares, this may well lead to the petition failing. This is largely because in the event of a successful petition, the most common remedy will be for the court to order a buy-out of the petitioner's shares. One of the main reasons why the unfair prejudice remedy is needed is because it is often very difficult for shareholders in private limited companies to sell their shares.

10.6 Remedies for unfair prejudice

Although the most common remedy is a buy-out, the court has a very broad discretion to make whatever order it sees fit; this means that the courts can be very flexible.

2 The law in this area is dominated by the judgment of Lord Hoffman in *O'Neill v Phillips* [1999] UKHL 24.
3 *Ebrahimi v Westbourne Galleries* [1970] AC 360.

10.7 Derivative action

Derivative actions are so-called because the right to sue is derived from the company's right to sue. Members can sue and so can people who are not yet members but to whom shares have been transferred or transmitted by operation of law. (For example, through bankruptcy or death of a member.)

A claim may be brought for an actual or proposed act or omission involving negligence, default, breach of duty, or breach of trust by a director of the company.

10.8 Permission to continue claim

There are hurdles that a claimant must overcome before the court will consider the substance of the claim. These are in place to prevent spurious claims from vexatious litigants. There are two stages.

- First is an application where the claimant must file evidence to establish a *prima facie* case. If there is no *prima facie* case the court must dismiss.
- Second, the court assesses whether the claim should proceed based on both mandatory and discretionary factors.

10.9 Mandatory factors

The court must dismiss the claim if:

> The court is satisfied that a person acting in accordance with S.172 *Companies Act 2006*, the duty to promote the success of the company (discussed in Chapter 8), would not continue it.
>
> Where the act complained of was authorised or ratified by the company.

10.10 Discretionary factors

Under S.263 (3) *Companies Act 2006*, the court must consider the following non-exhaustive list of factors when deciding whether to allow the claim to continue:

- Whether the person was acting in good faith in bringing the claim.
- The importance that someone acting in accordance with S.172 *Companies Act 2006* would attach to continuing.
- Potential for ratification or authorisation.
- Whether the company had decided not to pursue the claim.
- Whether the member could bring an action in a different way.

10.11 Just and equitable winding up

Before the unfair prejudice petition came into widespread use, often the only way for a wronged shareholder to get redress from a company was the just and equitable winding-up procedure that can be used largely under similar principles to those under which an unfair prejudice petition can be brought. As the name suggests, this remedy is a bit of a blunt instrument and will result in the demise of the company. It is possible to bring an action for just and equitable winding up at the same time as an unfair prejudice petition.

10.12 Contractual self-help remedies

Thinking ahead is the key thing here. By placing clauses in articles of association and shareholders' agreements focused on what might happen in the event of business partners falling out or simply wishing to retire earlier than envisaged, directors and shareholders can in many cases obviate the need for expensive and protracted litigation further down the line. There are a wide number of contractual options including:

- Service contracts.
- Weighted voting clauses in the articles of association.
- Buy-out clauses including mechanisms for valuing shares.
- Pre-emption rights.
- Clauses permitting transfer of shares/not permitting transfer of shares.
- Voting rights or requirements.

10.13 Commercial awareness talking point

The most important point to make about litigation within the company is that it is very expensive, often ruinously so for a company. It is nearly always better to secure agreements outside court and to avoid derivative actions and unfair prejudice petitions entirely.

It is good advice to give any client setting up a company that problems often arise and good relations between shareholders cannot be guaranteed long term. Shareholders should consider very carefully what provisions they could include in a shareholders' agreement or the articles of association that may protect their positions.

Chapter 10 revision points

- Minority shareholders are potentially vulnerable in private limited companies if they are not happy with how the company is being run.
- Due to the structure of company law and the underlying principle of majority rule, it is often very difficult and costly to bring an action against the board for

mismanagement or other breaches of directors' duties. These problems are exacerbated in private limited companies where there is no available market for shares and often restrictions on share transfers.

- The unfair prejudice petition is an action that can be brought by members of a private limited company if their interests have been unfairly prejudiced. Although the legislation is drafted broadly, the courts usually only find there has been unfair prejudice if there has been a breach of a shareholder's contractual rights or the strict imposition of a corporate rule which ignored a mutual understanding of how the company was to be run.
- The main remedy under an unfair prejudice petition is an order that the company or the majority buy the shares of the prejudiced member – unfair prejudice is really an exit strategy from the company. Unfair prejudice petitions are only usually successful in smaller private limited companies where it is difficult to transfer shares.
- The derivative action enables shareholders to bring an action on behalf of the company against a director or directors, usually for breach of duty.
- There is a staged process where the permission to continue the claim must be sought after a *prima facie* case has been established.
- The principle of majority rule is still strong in this area and derivative actions will not succeed if the act complained of has been ratified by an independent majority of shareholders.

PART 3 Partnerships

11 Ordinary partnerships

11.1 Chapter overview

The phrase "ordinary" or "general" partnerships refers to partnerships that are governed by the *Partnership Act 1890* and the case law relating to partnerships. Ordinary partnerships are not registered at Companies House and do not have a separate legal personality. This chapter looks at key aspects of partnership law and practice. Ordinary partnerships are very common business forms in the UK, and they are likely to feature strongly in the Business Law and Practice element of SQE1 & SQE2.

Partners have considerable flexibility over how their partnerships operate, and they can tailor their partnership agreements to suit themselves. In many respects, the *Partnership Act 1890* largely consists of a set of default rules that will apply unless the partners have agreed otherwise.

11.2 Formation of a partnership

Partnership is defined under the *Partnership Act 1890* as "the relation which subsists between persons carrying on a business in common with a view of profit".[1]

The components are considered below.

11.2.1 "Relation"

Partnership is based on a contractual relationship and many partnerships will have formal written agreements. It is common for agreements to be oral also and in some circumstances the courts can even imply an agreement that the partners are not aware that they have made. Where the partners have not agreed their own terms, they are bound by the default rules of the *Partnership Act 1890*.

11.2.2 "Between persons"

This now means two or more (there is no upper limit). Note that persons can include registered Ltd companies and LLP partnerships.

1 *S.1 Partnership Act 1890.*

DOI: 10.4324/9781003289760-14

11.2.3 "Business in common"

Under the PA 1890 business includes "every trade, occupation, or profession."[2] It is not a requirement that the business has started trading but the partners must have done something preparatory to set up the enterprise.

11.2.4 "With a view of profit"

The intention to share profits is a key feature of a partnership and agreement to share profits is *prima facie,* although not conclusive, evidence that a partnership exists. There is no requirement that a profit is made in fact, but there must be the intention that a profit will be made. It must also be possible to make a profit, so an agreement between parties to contrive to create a loss may well not satisfy the requirement.

11.3 Partnership agreements and common terms

If there is no partnership agreement in place, the default provisions of the *Partnership Act 1890* will apply. This can have consequences that partners may not be happy with. To avoid these consequences, the following terms are regularly in partnership agreements.

11.3.1 Commencement

Although the start date of the partnership could depend on the facts and when exactly the conditions of partnership arise, there is great value in partners setting a date for commencement. A stipulated date can demonstrate a contractual intention to commence on a particular date. The benefit from this is some degree of certainty for the parties about when their potential liabilities or obligations commence.

11.3.2. Duration of partnership/dissolution of partnership

A partnership will either be for a specified time, or it will be a partnership at will. Because a partnership at will can be terminated by one partner giving notice a clause is often inserted ensuring it is not a partnership at will (for example stating that the partnership can only be terminated according to another provision of the agreement). A common clause to include would be that the partnership does not automatically terminate if a partner retires or becomes bankrupt.

11.3.3 Partnership capital

The agreement will normally contain a statement of the partners' initial capital contributions to the firm. Unless there is anything to the contrary in the agreement, partners cannot be compelled to invest further sums.

2 S.45 *Partnership Act 1890.*

11.3.4 Partnership property

A partnership, in England and Wales, does not have a separate legal personality. This means that the expression "partnership property" is potentially misleading. It is common for partners to use their personal assets for the benefit of the partnership. Where this happens, ownership of the asset should be specified in the partnership agreement as this can lead to disputes later.

11.3.5 Sharing profits and losses

Under the *Partnership Act 1890* partners share all profits and losses equally. Unless the partners have contributed equally to both workload and investment, this will not be an ideal situation. Commonly a partnership agreement will be adapted to pay a greater share of income profits to partners who have put more hours in and share capital profits according to the share of capital each partner has invested.

11.3.6 Roles/responsibilities in the partnership

Under the *Partnership Act 1890* all partners are entitled to take part in the management of the partnership, but there is no requirement that they do. The concept of a sleeping partner is well known, and it is common for some partners to have an investment role but no active role in management. The partnership agreement is a good way to set out partners' various responsibilities in the partnership (full-time commitment if appropriate).

11.3.7 Expulsion/removal of partner

There is no power under the *Partnership Act 1890* to remove a partner; therefore partnership agreements often contain clauses under which a partner can be removed by a specified majority (often 75%) in certain circumstances.

11.3.8 Decision-making in the partnership

Under the *Partnership Act 1890* decision-making is on a majority basis apart from the following situations, which need the unanimous consent of the partners:

- The introduction of a new partner.
- A change in the nature of the partnership business.
- A change to the partnership agreement.

It is open to the partners to require more decisions to be made unanimously, or with an enhanced majority.

11.4 Liability of partners in an ordinary partnership

The most important difference between ordinary partnerships and companies is that partners do not have limited liability. Partners are jointly and severally liable for all the debts of the partnership. Partners can also be liable for tortious acts committed by a partner.

11.5 When does a partner cease to be liable for debts of the partnership?

- **Debts incurred while someone is a partner**

  A partner can be liable for any debts incurred during the time when they were a partner. To avoid debts incurred during the partnership period, the firm's creditors would need to enter into a novation agreement to transfer the contractual obligations to the new partners. In practice this is very uncommon. More commonly, the continuing partners can indemnify the retiring partner.
- **Debts incurred after a partner has retired**

  To avoid liability for debts after the partner has retired, those dealing with the firm need to have actual notice of the partner's retirement.

  For those who have not so far dealt with the partnership, notification is deemed to have happened if an advert is placed in the *London Gazette*.

  Provided notice requirements have been fulfilled, a retiring partner will avoid liability for future debts providing they are not liable through holding out.

11.6 Liability through holding out

Even if someone is no longer a partner, it is possible that they can be held liable for partnership debts if they have been "held out" as a partner, either by themselves or by others (but with the person's knowledge.)

The holding out can be in writing, oral or by conduct.

11.7 Liability in tort

Partners in a firm can be liable in negligence for torts committed by another partner in the course of the partnership business or with the authority of the partners.

11.8 Power to bind the firm

A partner can enter contracts that bind the firm if that partner has the authority. This authority can be actual (express or implied) or apparent.

Express actual authority is when a partner has been expressly given authority to enter the contract or this *kind* of contract. Implied actual authority is inferred from conduct and the course of dealing. If there are no limitations agreed between the partners on their powers to bind the firm, actual authority will be implied.

Apparent authority is where a person who lacks actual authority may appear to have authority to a third party. The firm can be bound when a person acts with apparent authority in the following circumstances:

- The person is acting in the usual way business is carried on by the firm.
- The third party does not know that the partner does not have actual authority.
- The third party knows or believes that the person is a partner of the firm.

11.9 Fiduciary duties owed by partners to each other

Partners owe fiduciary duties to each other. These duties are very similar to those owed by directors to their companies, discussed elsewhere in Chapter 8.

Partners owe a duty of good faith to each other. Although this is not explicitly stated in statute, this duty is long recognised in case law and is also implicit in areas of the *Partnership Act 1890*.

Partners have a duty to ensure that their own interests and their duties to the other partners do not conflict and a duty not to make secret profits.

The *Partnership Act 1890* sets out the following duties in s.28-30, all of which derive from the fiduciary duties above.

- Duty to render accounts.
- Duty to account for private profits
- Duty not to compete with the partnership

11.10 Duty of care and skill owed by partners to each other

Partners also owe a duty of care and skill. The exact scope of this duty remains unclear. The historical case law in this area refers to a duty to act "without culpable negligence"[3] and this was later refined to mean that a partner should not act "below the standards of a reasonable businessman in the situation in which he found himself."[4]

The uncertain nature and scope of the duty of care and skill suggests that it may not feature significantly in SQE1.

11.11 Commercial awareness talking points

The clear message with partnerships is the importance of having a partnership agreement to avoid some of the default rules of the *Partnership Act 1890*. The following table sets out some of the default provisions and suggests suitable clauses that counteract the effect of the *Partnership Act 1890*.

3 *Bury v Allen* (1845) 1 Coll 589, 604.
4 *Winsor v Schroeder* (1979) 129 NLJ 1266.

Default provision in the Partnership Act 1890	Potential partnership agreement clause
Partners share equally in the capital and profits of the business and contribute equally towards the losses whether of capital or otherwise sustained by the firm.	Common clauses will link the entitlement to capital to the capital investment of each partner. Share in income profits can also be linked to work input in the firm.
Where there is a partnership at will, any partner may determine the partnership at any time on giving notice of his intention so to do to all the other partners.	Clauses commonly exclude a partner's right to terminate the partnership. Clauses can ensure it is not a partnership at will; for example, by stating that the partnership will continue for the duration of the joint lives of the partners. Clauses can also stipulate when and how the partnership can be dissolved.
No power to expel partners from partnership.	Clauses sometimes give a specified majority of partners the power to remove a partner in specified circumstances. (Breach of partnership agreement or other duty.)
No partner entitled to remuneration for acting for the partnership.	A clause can give a partner the right to a salary.
Majority decision-making in all but three areas where unanimity is needed: Change of partnership business. Introduction of new partners. Change of partnership agreement.	A clause could be included to require enhanced majorities or unanimity in other key areas.
Every partner may take part in the management of the partnership, but there is no requirement that they do.	A clause setting out respective responsibilities of partners, in particular time commitment – part-time, full-time, for example.

Chapter 11 revision points

- General or ordinary partnerships are regulated by the *Partnership Act 1890* and the common law rules relating to partnerships.
- General partnerships are not registered at Companies House.
- Partners are jointly and severally liable for all the debts of the partnership.
- Partnerships do not have a separate legal personality.
- A written partnership agreement is not required by law, but it is advisable if partners want to avoid the application of any of the default rules in the *Partnership Act 1890*.

12 Limited liability partnerships

12.1 Chapter overview

This chapter considers limited liability partnerships in a little more depth. LLPs are organisations that are hybrid in nature, sharing many of the same characteristics of both private limited companies and ordinary partnerships. The chapter looks at formation requirement, the role and responsibilities of designated members, before considering the similarities with other business forms in more detail. The commercial awareness section focuses on the advantages and disadvantages of the LLP form compared to other business organisations

12.2 Formation of an LLP

The incorporation of an LLP requires:

- Two or more associated people. The "people" can include an incorporated company. There is no upper limit for the number of members.
- As with ordinary partnerships, the members must be carrying on a lawful business with a view to profit.
- The members must subscribe their names to an incorporation document which must be delivered to the registrar at Companies House.
- The incorporation document is essentially the form LL IN01 which requires similar information to be filed (detailed below.)
- A solicitor or anyone subscribing to the LL IN01 must sign a statement confirming compliance with the requirements of registration.

12.3 Content of LL IN01

The following information is required on the LL IN01 form.

- The name of the LLP.
- Location of office (England and Wales, Wales, Scotland, or Northern Ireland).
- Address of registered office.
- Designated members – either all members are designated or at least two members must be designated.

DOI: 10.4324/9781003289760-15

- Members' names, country of residence, month and year of birth, and whether they are a designated member.
- Member's service address.
- Member's date of birth – this does not get shown on the public record.
- Member's usual residential address – this page does not get shown on the public record.
- Corporate member appointments.
- Confirmation that there is or is not someone with significant control over the LLP
- Name and address of persons with significant control or registrable relevant legal entities.

12.4 Role of designated members

There must be two designated members. If there are only two members, then they are automatically the designated members.

Designated members have various responsibilities including maintaining accounting records, appointing auditors, and preparing, signing, and filing accounts at Companies House.

12.5 Comparison with ordinary partnerships

One of the main reasons for the introduction of LLPs was to provide professional firms such as accountants the opportunity to form business organisations that had both separate legal personality and also limited liability. (Until fairly recently many professional firms were prevented from operating as limited companies by their professional regulatory bodies.) Although many professional firms now have much greater freedom as to which business form to use (and often adopt the form of a limited company), the LLP remains a popular business form that has many of the advantages of both an ordinary partnership and a limited company.

Although the Limited Liability Partnerships Act makes clear that the general law of partnership does not apply to LLPs, unless stipulated otherwise in the Act, there are still a great number of similarities. Similarly, there is a significant overlap with company law as some of the *Companies Act 2006* also applies to LLPs.

12.6 Similar default provisions

LLPs have many similarities with ordinary partnerships. If the members do not agree otherwise the following default provisions will apply from the respective Acts.

- All members/partners are entitled to share equally in the capital and profits of the LLP/ordinary partnership.

- The LLP/firm must indemnify each member/partner in respect of payments made and personal liabilities incurred by him –
  a) In the ordinary and proper business of the LLP/firm; or
  b) In or about anything necessarily done for the preservation of the business or property of the LLP/firm.
- Every member/partner may take part in the management of the LLP/partnership business.
- No member/partner is entitled to remuneration for acting in the business or management of the LLP or in the partnership business.
- Decisions between members/partners will be made by majority, apart from the decisions to introduce new members or to change the nature of the partnership business which require the consent of all members/partners.
- The partnership books must be kept at the registered office of the LLP (or such place as the members see fit)/place of business of the partnership, and any member/partner may have access to them and inspect and copy them.
- Although it is strongly recommended, there is no legal requirement for a written partnership agreement.
- The tax treatment of LLPs is the same as ordinary partnerships. For example, although LLPs have corporate personalities, they do not pay corporation tax.

12.7 Commercial awareness talking point

The LLP is clearly a hybrid form that has characteristics of companies and partnerships. The key company similarity is the requirements for registration at Companies House and the various publicity requirements – however, it is notable that these requirements differ between the two and this may mean that it is a nuanced decision about what form is most suitable.

Chapter 12 revision points

- LLPs are registered at Companies House.
- Members have limited liability.
- LLPs have separate legal personality.
- LLPs have many of the characteristics of companies and partnerships.
- There are differences in tax treatment and publicity requirements that may make forming an LLP more or less attractive to a businessperson.

PART

4 Business accounts and tax

13 Calculating business profits

Rachel Cooper

13.1 Chapter overview

Solicitors are better placed to give advice where they have a knowledge of how business profits are calculated and where they understand the nature of tax reliefs and allowances that can be claimed by businesses. An awareness of the types of profit and the types of accounting information that are produced will support solicitors in fulfilling their roles; this applies to accounting information that is used for statutory as well as commercial purposes.

This chapter looks at how business profits are calculated, and consideration is given to the types of profit that can be identified in businesses. The chapter explores what allowances can be claimed to offset against tax liabilities as well as consideration of tax relief in the event of a business being loss-making. Accounting systems and the information that is produced from them, along with the purposes of that information, are explained.

13.2 Why is calculating profits important?

Privately owned businesses, of all types, exist to make a financial return to owners and to service wider stakeholders. An awareness of the financial health of a business is crucial so that owners and wider stakeholders can make decisions appropriately. In other words, stakeholders need to know what the financial performance of a business is as well as its financial position. Profit will be calculated for each accounting period (usually a financial year) to establish performance and this calculation must be produced in a consistent, understandable, and verifiable way. The ability of stakeholders to establish a reliable profit figure is essential to support their decision-making. Those owning a business are interested in what the returns on their investment in the business are; those managing the business will want to understand if their decisions and actions have been successful. By law, businesses must pay taxation and a clearly defined and accurately calculated profit will be an essential part of legally compliant tax calculations which will be required by HMRC (His Majesty's Revenue and Customs, the tax collecting authority in the UK).

DOI: 10.4324/9781003289760-17

13.3 Types of profit

There are two key types of profit: one is profit generated from income, usually made up of trading profit, and the second is profit generated as a result of changes in capital items. While profit from income is usually made up of trading profit there may be additional income such as that from the rental of a property.

The distinction between income and capital profits is important for two reasons. First, it is necessary for accurate reporting of performance to stakeholders, for example through statutory annual financial statements. Second, defining profit is a first step in making tax calculations.

13.4 Income profits

Income profits are recurring in nature and are generated over repeated timescales. They can include daily sales revenue from trading, regular weekly expenditure on raw materials, or monthly income for property rental. All recurring items can be aggregated to provide information on income profits generated over longer time periods such as a 12-month financial year.

13.5 Capital profits

Capital profits are known by HMRC as chargeable gains and these are derived from transactions concerning capital items such as physical assets such as plant and machinery, or financial assets such as stocks and shares in another company. By nature, they are one-off items.

13.6 Calculating income profits

Taxation calculations vary depending on the type of business organisation and will relate to income tax in the case of a sole trader or partnership, and to corporation tax in the case of an incorporated company. While there is no clear definition of income or exactly what is meant by chargeable receipts, it is generally taken that this is income received as part of the expected trading activity of the business.

Profit from income is largely made from trading in goods or services but it is possible to have further income from other sources, for example rental income or income from investments. Trading profit is calculated by taking the difference between income generated from goods and services sold to customers (traded) and the expenditure incurred because of that trading, that is, the costs incurred in the production and provision of those goods and services.

Simply put, the output from the business which is sold to customers (be those end consumers or other businesses), minus the expenditure incurred to produce/provide that output, is trading profit.

Trading profits are calculated in essentially the same way for income tax or corporation tax purposes and are made up of chargeable receipts (revenue generated) and deductible expenses (expenses incurred that are allowable for tax purposes). HMRC also allows for the deduction of capital allowances to recognise the use of assets when deriving trading profit.

Deductible expenses are those expenses that are incurred wholly and exclusively in the normal course of trade, for example the purchase of raw materials which will be used and transformed into a final product. Not all expenditure items are permitted, such as expenses incurred in entertaining clients, or costs associated with leasing high emission cars.

The following formula helps to define clearly what is meant by trading profits (or losses):

Trading Profit/Loss = Chargeable Receipts – Deductible Expenditure – Capital Allowances.

13.7 Calculating capital profits

Capital items are the long-standing physical assets or financial resources upon which the trade relies. Capital profits are profits generated on the sale of a capital item. Profit is calculated by finding the difference between the cost of the asset and the value received for it when sold.

To work this out, a business will usually take the value of the asset when it was sold as being the amount that was received for it. The amount that was paid for the asset initially is usually deducted from the amount received and further expenditure that was incurred in buying, selling, or improving that asset will also be deducted. HMRC allow for an Indexation Allowance for older assets to be applied to allow for the effects of inflation. The indexation allowance recognises that not all of the gain in the value of an asset over time should be regarded as profit; some of the gain will be due to the effects of inflation. The application of the allowance results in a smaller gain being included in the tax calculation which reduces the amount of tax due.

13.8 Capital allowances

Businesses can claim capital allowances on plant and machinery which are acquired to produce the output of goods and services. These allowances relate to capital items and not items purchased for resale. Essentially, plant and machinery refers to all the goods and chattels that are used on a permanent basis in the business. Businesses can deduct some, or all, of the value of these capital items from profits before tax is calculated and paid, using capital allowances as defined by HMRC. Through capital allowances HMRC recognise the "using up" of the economic value of assets; a recognition that assets depreciate (reduce in value) over time, and when being used in the course of business. On the other hand, when accountants calculate trading profits to report to shareholders and other users, a similar depreciation charge is made to profits to reflect the using up of assets. The method of calculation of this accounting depreciation is driven by professional accounting standards and is calculated in a different way to capital allowances. HMRC require that accounting depreciation is removed from calculations and is replaced by capital allowances to find taxable profit. This way, HMRC can influence and incentivise the purchase of assets.

There are two allowances that can be claimed. The Annual Investment Allowance (AIA) allows companies to claim, within the AIA annual limit, the full cost of new plant and machinery purchased, except for business cars. If the AIA limit is reached, a company can additionally claim Writing Down Allowances (WDA).

Each financial year, a business will be able to claim AIA and WDA; the amount calculated will be deducted from chargeable receipts to calculate trading profits upon which tax will be charged. The WDA recognises the concept of depreciation – the notion that an asset reduces in value over time. As mentioned above, depreciation is an accounting adjustment to reflect the economic use of assets and to match the value used of an asset to the income generated from its use. Depreciation charged in the statutory accounting statements is not allowable in the calculation of tax-adjusted trading profits; it is not a deductible expenditure; capital allowances are given instead in tax computations.

Currently the AIA maximum is £1 million, and the WDA is a percentage of the value of the qualifying plant and machinery the business owns and will be calculated annually; currently this is 18% on the value of plant and machinery. The WDA is deducted from the value of the assets, after AIA is taken.

Companies use a system of "pooling" assets such that they can then apply appropriate allowances and rates to assets as grouped together in "pools". This saves a complex procedure that would involve working out the capital allowance for each individual item. Pooling simply means collating and keeping records for a group of assets with like characteristics, and rates for different pools are set by HMRC. The 18% WDA, as previously stated, relates to main pool plant and machinery.

13.9 Capital allowances: A worked example

A business started trading in Year 1 and the following schedule shows the first two years of capital allowances. Notice how the additions of assets attract allowances for annual investment (AIA), to a maximum of £1 million for qualifying assets, as well as a written-down value allowance of 18% on the pool of assets that remain after the AIA has been taken. Also notice how the value of the main pool of assets reduces over time and this effectively allows the business to deduct the value of the qualifying assets from its trading profits over the course of several years; little or no tax is therefore paid on this expenditure; tax is paid, however, on any gains realised on later sales of the assets (as per Section 13.7).

		Main pool	Allowances
Year 1	£	£	£
Additions:			
Plant and machinery	1,250,000		
Office furniture and equipment	150,000		
	1,400,000		
AIA used (up to a max of £1 million)	(1,000,000)		1,000,000
Remainder after AIA		400,000	
Main pool value		400,000	
Apply WDA (18%)		(72,000)	72,000
Total WDV carried forward to Year 2		**328,000**	
Total Allowances Year 1			**1,072,000**
		Main pool	**Allowances**
Year 2	£	£	£
Total WDV brought forward from Year 1		328,000	
Additions:			
Plant and machinery	900,000		
Office furniture and equipment	10,000		
	910,000		
AIA used (up to a max of £1 million)	(910,000)		910,000
Remainder after AIA		0	
Main pool value		328,000	
Apply WDA (18%)		(59,040)	59,040
Total WDV carried forward to Year 3		**268,960**	
Total Allowances Year 2			**969,040**

In Year 1 trading profits would be reduced by £1,072,000 before tax is calculated and in Year 2 by £969,040.

13.10 Accounting periods

When the term "accounting period" is used, this usually relates to the accounting period of a trading entity such as a company. The accounting period is usually 12 months and is often called the financial year. Trading profits or losses are calculated relating to a financial year. The main exception to this is when a business starts trading and their financial year falls within the 12 months to the financial year end, from the commencement of trade. Once a business is up and running for more than a year a set of accounting statements are prepared for each sequence of 12 months of trading. The three main accounting statements are the Income Statement, the Statement of Financial Position (or Balance Sheet), and the Statement of Cash Flows and all are prepared to fit with the accounting period for a business, usually, as stated, 12 months.

There are other accounting periods in different contexts. For example, VAT returns are produced every three months, and this is known as the "accounting period" in this instance.

13.11 Relief for tax losses

Privately owned, commercial businesses aim to make a profit. This is where income from trading exceeds expenditure. It is entirely possible, however, that a business might make a loss with expenditure exceeding income. Where a trading loss is incurred, it can be possible to carry the loss forward to offset against future profits to reduce tax charges. Trading losses might also be claimed against income of current or previous accounting periods. There are factors that will influence the choice of how a loss relief claim might be made.

Carry forward loss relief will be used to deduct from profits of future accounting periods, as long as trade continues. A current year or a carry back relief must be made within a specified time period. Usually, any carry back loss relief is set off against trading losses of the previous 12 months with the losses to be set against profits of the most recent years first, but at the time or writing this has been extended to three years to provide further support to businesses post pandemic. It is more usual for this to be required to be claimed within the 12-month period ending immediately before the beginning of the loss-making accounting period.

Companies make decisions on when to take the relief for the tax loss by considering tax rates. This is to reduce the tax burden as much as possible. The company will also consider cash flow. If the loss is carried back this is likely to result in a refund, whereas if it is carried forward this will result in a reduction in the future tax liability.

Companies can gain tax relief from Qualifying Charitable Donations (QCDs) and unrelieved QCDs cannot be carried forward, so the company will consider the best use of the QCD relief coupled with the loss relief to minimise tax liabilities. Where a company incurs a trading loss during the final 12 months of trading it is possible to make a carry back claim against profits of the preceding three years.

The taxpayer can set off any trading losses against capital gains in the same tax year. This further relief is rather unusual in the sense that it allows loss relief against chargeable capital gains as well as against trading income.

13.12 Accounting information and systems

The role of accountants in business is to maintain financial records and prepare financial statements in accordance with statute but also to support the decision-making within the business. HMRC will require the accounts to be presented and a tax computation to be prepared, based on making adjustments for items chargeable or allowable for tax purposes. There is also a legal requirement to submit a copy of statutory accounting statements to Companies House where businesses are incorporated as limited companies. Larger businesses will employ accountants to work inside the organisation while many small and medium enterprises will appoint a firm of accountants to do this work for them. In either scenario the annual accounts must be audited by a firm of registered auditors to verify that the financial statements have been prepared appropriately and a statement to that effect must be included in the submission of annual statements to Companies House. The Director's Report similarly forms part of the statutory requirements of the *Companies Act 2006*. Failure to comply with requirements is a criminal offence.

To ensure that accounting information is consistent and comparable, accounting statements are produced in accordance with accounting standards. The Financial Reporting Council (FRC) is responsible for the setting of Financial Reporting Standards and for the oversight of auditing activities in the UK. The FRC is due to be replaced by the Audit, Reporting & Governance Authority (ARGA) by the end of 2024.

Accounting standards support businesses in calculating their profit by defining and guiding what is to be included as income and as expenditure and the accounting treatment of various categories of both. Accounting standards also help businesses to clearly define their financial position by defining and guiding the valuation of assets, liabilities, and capital. Accounting profit differs from taxable profit and, in essence, this is due to accounting adjustments such as the charging of depreciation of assets to profit, which is not allowable under tax calculations of profit. Instead of depreciation, capital allowances are included in the tax calculation of profit as discussed earlier in the chapter.

Accountants have a system which helps to ensure the accurate recording of financial transactions, and this is called double-entry bookkeeping. This essentially means that each financial transaction is recorded twice in the books of account. This acts as a cross-checking process to help improve accuracy and completeness. The accounts are said to be recorded in books as historically accounts were kept in large leather-bound books known as ledgers. In today's digital world even the smallest of companies is most likely to keep electronic records of accounting transactions and there are many specialist software apps and programmes to assist with the keeping of electronic ledgers.

The three primary statements produced from the accounting system for annual submission to Companies House are the Income Statement, the Statement of Financial Position (or Balance Sheet), and the Statement of Cash Flows. The Income Statement is prepared to reflect the performance over the accounting period (usually 12 months) and the Statement of Financial Position is prepared to reflect the financial position of the company as at the final day of the accounting period. The Statement of Cash Flows presents information to show from where cash has been generated and where it has been spent; it explains the movement in the cash position at the start of the period compared to that at the end. These statements have been identified earlier in the chapter in the context of taxation but are used widely by all stakeholders to understand the financial performance and position of a business. Other outputs for accounting information systems relate largely to management accounting which supports the managing of a business. The format, frequency, and presentation of such information is entirely discretionary, unlike statutory accounting information.

13.13 Commercial awareness talking point

To provide services to clients effectively, solicitors will have a knowledge of the legal requirements for the provision of accounting information and are well placed when they have a working knowledge of the uses and nature of accounting information more broadly. Being able to apply such knowledge to client-based and ethical problems will help solicitors to support clients appropriately and with confidence. Financial records and information, and accounting requirements, all form part of an understanding of the way business accounts are prepared and used. Knowledge of how trading profits are calculated and the implications for taxation are crucial such that solicitors can provide appropriate services to clients. Each client will present with different specific contexts, but the underlying principles of accounting information preparation and the rules of taxation are the same within any particular jurisdiction.

Chapter 13 revision points

- There are different types of profit – trading profit and capital profit being the main distinction.
- Profits are initially made as an accounting calculation and must be adjusted for tax purposes to provide a taxable profit in tax computations.
- There are allowances for tax relief, and these relate to capital purchases and to losses that a business may incur in an accounting period.
- The accounting period for which final accounting statements must legally be prepared is 12 months for an established trading entity.
- For an entity that has started part way through their financial year, this period will be fewer months.
- Other accounting periods can be established for other purposes such as management accounting.
- Information can be drawn from the accounting system for both internal and external purposes.

14 Income tax

14.1 Chapter overview

The UK government collects taxes from individuals and businesses every year. The SQE curriculum for Business Law and Practice includes income tax, capital gains tax, corporation tax, and value-added tax (VAT). Other taxes such as inheritance tax and stamp duty land tax are also features of the SQE curriculum in other areas.

This chapter looks at income tax, the tax that most of the public will have to pay at some point during their lives. Although expert detailed advice on taxation matters is usually left to trained accountants or tax-law specialists, newly qualified solicitors do need to be aware of the potential liabilities for various forms of taxation and how the taxation is calculated.

The chapter looks at what income actually is, who is liable to pay it, the various rates of income tax, and the steps involved in calculating income tax.

This chapter also considers various anti-avoidance measures and the modern judicial approach to statutory interpretation of taxation statutes.

14.2 What is income tax charged on?

Income is a concept that is very difficult to explain with precision, which probably explains why it is not defined in legislation. The essence of income, as opposed to other received payments, is the regularity with which income is received. For example, regular payment for employment would clearly be considered income whereas the proceeds from a one-off sale of property would most likely not.

Although the word "income" is not defined, the *Income Tax Act 2007* (as amended) details various types of income that income tax is charged on. For the purpose of the SQE and this book we will consider the following:

- Employment income.
- Pension income.

DOI: 10.4324/9781003289760-18

- Trading income.
- Property income.
- Savings and investment income.
- Miscellaneous income.

14.3 Who pays income tax?

Individuals pay income tax in a number of capacities. This most commonly means employees where tax is often deducted at source by the employer under the PAYE system.

An individual operating as a sole trader or sole practitioner will pay income tax as will personal representatives and trustees.

Individuals who are partners in a partnership pay income tax, but corporate partners do not. Companies, as separate legal personalities, do not pay income tax (or capital gains tax) but pay corporation tax instead. Shareholders of companies, as individuals, pay income tax on dividend payments.

14.4 The tax year

Income tax is paid on income earned in the tax year which starts on 6 April and ends on 5 April.

14.5 Rates of income tax

Tax rates are set by government and are subject to change. There are different tax rates for non-savings/non-dividends income, savings income, and dividends income.

There is a sliding scale of liability meaning that, in theory at least, those earning the most will pay a greater amount of income tax, both in total and proportionately.

14.6 Calculating income tax

S.23 *Income Tax Act 2007* details seven steps to calculate income tax liability:

1. **"Identify the amounts of income on which the taxpayer is charged to income tax for the tax year."**
   This could include:
   - Profits from trading.
   - Profits from savings and investments in interest and/or dividends.
   - Income from employment and pensions.
   - Income from property (for example rental income.)

The legislation refers to amounts of income as components. At this stage of the calculation these components need to be kept separate in the calculation as there are differences in how each income type's liability is calculated.

2. **"Deduct from the components the amount of any relief under a provision listed in relation to the taxpayer in Section 24 to which the taxpayer is entitled for the tax year."**

   The most common relief that solicitors should be aware of is the tax relief on the interest payments on qualifying loans. Such loans can include:
   - Loans to buy shares in private limited companies.
   - Loans to acquire an interest in a partnership (either LLP or general partnership.)
   - Loans to provide finance to a partnership.
   - Loans to buy equipment or machinery to a partnership.

   Normal business overdrafts and credit card purchases will not be classified as qualifying loans.

   After any reliefs have been deducted in Step2, the sum of the components left is called "net income".
3. **"Deduct from the amounts of the components left after Step 2 any allowances to which the taxpayer is entitled for the tax year under Chapter 2 of Part 3 of this Act ... 1 (individuals: personal allowance and blind person's allowance)."**
   - The current personal allowance for individuals is £12,570. This means that individuals can earn £12,570 without paying income tax. People with taxable income over £100,000 will have their personal allowance reduced by £1 for every £2 over £100,000. To calculate income tax liability, the personal allowance needs to be deducted from income in the following order:
     1. Against non-savings/non-dividends income.
     2. Against savings income (if the remaining allowance has not been used up on 1).
     3. Against dividends (if the remaining allowance has not been used on 1 and 2).
   - The personal savings allowance and the dividend allowance are distinct from the personal allowance and are treated differently. Rather than being straightforward deductions from income at this stage, these allowances are calculated when the rate of tax is applied. With a basic rate taxpayer, the first £1,000 is charged at a nil rate and with a higher rate taxpayer the first £500 is charged at a nil rate.
   - The first £2,000 of a taxpayer's dividend income is tax-free. This applies to taxpayers in all tax bands. This means that no tax will be paid by anyone on the dividends of £2,000 or under.
4. **"Calculate tax at each applicable rate on the amounts of the components left after Step 3."**

   Non-savings/non-dividends income is taxed first, then interest on savings, and then dividends. Rates of taxation are as below (note that rates change regularly):

Non-savings/non-dividends income	Basic rate 20%	£12,571–£50,270
	Higher rate 40%	£50,271–£150,000
	Additional rate 45%	Above £150,000
Savings	Starting rate 0% (Available only if other income is under £17,570) Personal Savings Allowance of £1,000 or £500 depending on the status of the tax payer (Basic Rate or Higher Rate) is available for savings income on top of the £5,000	£0–£5,000 Reduces by £1 for every £1 of other income above personal allowance (£12,570)
	Savings basic rate 20%	Up to £50,270
	Savings higher rate 40%	£50,271–£150,000
	Savings additional rate 45%	Over £150,000
Dividends	Basic rate 8.75%	Up to £50,270
	Higher rate 33.75%	£50,271–£150,000
	Additional rate 39.35%	Over £150,000

5. **Add together the amounts of tax calculated at Step 4.**
6. **Deduct from the amount of tax calculated at Step 5 any tax reductions to which the taxpayer is entitled for the tax year under a provision listed in relation to the taxpayer in Section 26.**

   There are a number of reductions that can be made at this stage that include:
   - Tax reductions for married couples and civil partners.
   - Relief for investors in venture capital schemes.
   - Relief for social investment.
   - Relief for non-deductible interest on loans to invest in partnership with residential property business.
   - Gift aid.
7. **Add to the amount of tax left after Step 6 any amounts of tax for which the taxpayer is liable for the tax year under any provision listed in relation to the taxpayer in Section 30.**

   The section refers to a number of items of additional tax including high-income child-benefit charge and an assortment of pension-scheme charges.

   The result of the calculation of Steps 1 to 7 is the taxpayer's liability to income tax for the tax year.

14.7 Tax calculation exercise

In the 2022/23 tax year a man receives the following payments:

- A gross salary of £20,000.
- £1,500 interest on a savings account.
- £3,000 in dividends from shares in a listed company on the London Stock Exchange.

- £20,000 on the sale of a vintage car that the man purchased for £10,000 seven years ago. The man is not a car dealer, and this is the only time he has sold a car.

Calculate the man's liability for income tax for 2022/23.

Answer:

Apply Steps 1 to 5 (as insufficient information – no need to apply Steps 6 and 7).

1. **Identify the amounts of income on which the taxpayer is charged to income tax for the tax year.**
   The salary is non-savings/non-dividend income: £20,000
   The interest is savings income: £1,500
   The dividend payments are dividend income: £3,000
   The profit on the car purchase is not income.
2. **Deduct from the components the amount of any relief.**
   As far as we know, there are no reliefs to deduct here.
3. **Deduct from the amounts of the components left any allowances.**
   Personal allowance is deducted from the salary: £20,000 – £12,570 = £7,430
4. **Calculate tax at each applicable rate on the amounts of the components left.**
   Salary (Non-Savings/Non-Dividends income) taxed at the basic rate:
   £7,430 @ 20% = £1,486
   Savings income taxed at the basic rate:
   £1,000 @ 0% = £0
   £500 @ 20% = £100
   Dividend income taxed at the basic rate:
   £2,000 @ 0% = £0
   £1,000 @ 8.75%= £87.50
5. **Add together amounts of tax calculated at Step 4.**
   £1,486 + £100 + £87.50 = £1,673.50
   On the information available the man's total liability for income tax for 2022/23 is £1,673.50.

14.8 Collection and payment

HMRC are responsible for the collection of taxation. For employed people this usually happens when tax is deducted at source under the PAYE system by employers on behalf of HMRC. The employee receives the salary net of tax (meaning the income tax has already been deducted.)

Where tax has not been deducted at source, the individual concerned needs to fill in a tax return on the HMRC self-assessment system.

Taxpayers are encouraged to file tax returns using the online system before 31 January following the end of the relevant tax year.

14.9 Anti-avoidance measures

There has always been an element of "cat and mouse" about the tax rules implemented by governments and the innovative measures that tax advisers put in place to reduce their clients' tax liabilities. Historically, case law actively supported the right of taxpayers to arrange their affairs as far as they could within the law to take advantage of any defects or omissions in tax statutes. This approach has changed significantly in recent years.

The legal system has now significantly changed with the enactment of the General Anti-Abuse Rule (GAAR).[1] A further point of relevance in this regard is the modern approach adopted by the courts known as the Ramsay principles of statutory interpretation.

14.10 The GAAR

14.10.1 Scope

The scope of the GAAR is significant for the SQE as the rules apply to all of the following taxes:

- Income tax.
- Capital gains tax.
- Inheritance tax.
- Corporation tax
- Stamp duty land tax.

14.10.2 Purpose

The purpose of the GAAR is to stop taxpayers from entering into abusive avoidance arrangements and to also deter their promotion. If a taxpayer does go ahead with an abusive arrangement, the GAAR is designed to enable HMRC to make "an appropriate tax adjustment that is just and reasonable in all the circumstances". The are no direct penalties under the GAAR – but obviously if the taxpayer does not consequently pay the adjusted amount there is the potential for penalties under other legislation.

14.10.3 Relation to other tax legislation

The GAAR takes priority over all other legislation relating to the relevant taxes.

14.10.4 What is an "abusive" avoidance arrangement?

To determine whether an arrangement is abusive a double-reasonableness test is applied. They are arrangements that "cannot reasonably be regarded as a reasonable course of action in relation to the relevant tax provisions, having regard to all the circumstances".[2]

1 Part 5, *Finance Act 2013*.
2 S.207(2) *Finance Act 2013*.

There is detailed published guidance from HMRC that gives further insights into what is an abusive arrangement.

14.11 The Ramsay principle of statutory interpretation

The modern approach to statutory interpretation in areas of tax stems from the seminal decision in Ramsay.[3] The Ramsay principle is an extension of the purposive approach where the courts look first to the intention of parliament when choosing the words of the statute and then consider the wider factual matrix to see whether an individual transaction can be considered in isolation or within a wider context.

14.12 Commercial awareness point

Great care should be taken in the area of taxation for newly qualified solicitors. Issues relating to taxation crop up on a very regular basis in many areas of practice and solicitors need to be mindful of the complex and constantly changing nature of tax law. A broad understanding of the potential liabilities for various forms of taxation is essential for all solicitors, but it will frequently be the case that a newly qualified solicitor will need expert guidance from legal or accounting professionals more well-versed in specific areas.

Chapter 14 revision points

- Income tax is charged on income.
- Income is not defined in the legislation but can be said to be payments with some form of regularity in nature.
- There are three distinct types of income: non-savings/non-dividends income, savings income, and dividends income.
- To calculate income tax liability, the legislation sets out seven steps.
- Income tax is collected by HMRC.
- Income tax is often deducted at source by an employer and paid to HMRC under the PAYE system.
- Income tax is otherwise declared in an online tax return by 31 January after the end of the relevant tax year.

3 *WT Ramsay Ltd v IRC* [1982] AC 300.

15 Capital gains tax

15.1 Chapter overview

The SQE curriculum refers to the following aspects of capital gains tax (CGT):

- Chargeable persons/entities (sole traders, partners, and shareholders).
- Basis of charge (calculation of gains/allowable deductions/main reliefs and exemptions).
- The charge to tax: calculation and collection.
- The scope of anti-avoidance provisions.

This chapter covers all these aspects apart from the anti-avoidance provisions that have been referred to already in Chapter 14.

The chapter concludes with a brief discussion about business relief for inheritance tax. Although inheritance tax is an area that forms part of the Wills, Trusts, and Estates part of the SQE curriculum it makes sense to consider this, as the relief is very similar to reliefs for CGT.

15.2 Chargeable persons

Individuals pay capital gains tax, often in the role of a sole trader, partner, or shareholder. The tax is paid on chargeable gains made from the disposal of chargeable assets.

15.3 Chargeable assets

Chargeable assets can be any form of property including:

- Personal possessions over a set value (currently £6,000).
- Land, not including an individual's main home.
- Shares that are not in an individual savings account (ISA) or a personal equity plan (PEP).
- Goodwill of a business.
- Contractual rights.

DOI: 10.4324/9781003289760-19

(It is possible that individuals may have to pay capital gains tax on the disposal of crypto assets – however, please note, there is no indication that these will feature in the SQE.)

15.4 Disposal of assets

This will often be a sale, but disposal has a broad meaning and can also include gifts, swaps, or even insurance pay-outs.

15.5 Gifts to spouses or civil partners

There are different rules for gifts to spouses and charities which mean that capital gains tax is usually not payable.

15.6 How to calculate CGT

The statute does not stipulate a method for calculating liability for CGT and there is no universally agreed method. It is common to apply the following stages:

1. Identify disposal of chargeable asset.
2. Calculate gain on disposal of chargeable asset.
3. Subtract allowable expenditure and indexation if appropriate.
4. Apply reliefs.
5. Deduct annual exemption.
6. Apply the relevant tax rate.

15.7 Calculate gain on disposal

In many cases the disposal is a sale, and the gain will be the difference between the sale price of the property in the disposal and the price for which it was initially purchased.

For example: If a man purchases an antique vase in 2017 for £20,000 and sells it to an antique dealer in 2020 for £28,000, the gain will be £8,000 (assuming there are no additional costs relating to the disposal.)

Where the disposal is a gift (other than to a spouse or a charity) the gain will the difference between the market value of the asset and the original amount that it was purchased.

For example: If a man purchases an antique violin in 2016 for £20,000 and gives the violin to a friend in 2019, the gain will be the difference between the market value of the violin in 2019 and £20,000.

There is often further expenditure that can be subtracted, for example:

1. Costs of acquisition and incidental costs of acquisition. As well as the cost price mentioned above, there can also be extra costs associated with the original purchase. In a standard purchase of a property this may include conveyancing and legal fees "...wholly and exclusively for the acquisition of the asset, together with the incidental costs to him of the acquisition, or, if the asset was not acquired by him, any expenditure wholly and exclusively incurred by him in providing the asset".[1]
2. Cost of expenditure wholly and exclusively incurred to enhance the value of the asset. For example, this could be a building of an extension on a property. This would not include regular maintenance.
3. Incidental costs of disposal incurred wholly and exclusively for the purpose of the disposal. This could include valuation costs or advertising costs to find a buyer.

15.8 Subtracting allowable expenditure

Certain expenditures can be deducted from the gain. In the case of a sale of a property, this would include money spent on an extension, but it would not include day-to-day repairs to the property.

Similarly, costs relating to the practicalities of the sale itself or the initial purchase, for example, agency fees can be deducted.

15.9 Indexation

In 1982, the indexation allowance was introduced to reflect the fact that a high period of inflation meant that gains were much larger than they would have been in times of lower inflation. The indexation allowance has not been in place since 2008. It is potentially still relevant to CGT calculations for certain roll-over and hold-over reliefs prior to April 2008 but it seems unlikely to feature strongly in the SQE curriculum.

15.10 Apply reliefs

It is possible to reduce or delay capital gains tax by applying some of the following reliefs:

- **Business asset rollover relief**

  The effect of this relief is to delay the payment of CGT on a disposal if all or part of the proceeds of the disposal are used on the purchase of a new asset.

  To be eligible for relief the following need to apply:

1 S.38 (1)(a) *Taxation of Capital Gains Act 1992.*

  - The new assets must be purchased within three years of the disposal of the old assets (or in the year prior to the disposal).
  - The business must be trading (when the assets are bought and sold).
  - The assets (bought and sold) must be used in the business.
- **Business asset disposal relief (until recently called entrepreneurs' relief)**

  This relief is sometimes available to those disposing of all or part of a business. Those qualifying for this relief will pay CGT at a reduced rate, currently 10%.

  For partners or sole traders to be eligible the following must apply:
  - The person claiming relief must have been a partner or sole trader for the past two years.
  - The person must have owned the business for the past two years.

  For those selling shares, the following must have been in place for the past two years:
  - The person claiming must be an officer or employee of the company or of the holding company.
  - The company must be a trading company or the holding company of a trading company.
  - The person claiming must hold 5% or more of the shares and the voting rights.
  - The person claiming must be entitled to 5% of the profits on a winding up or 5% of disposal proceeds if the business is sold.
- **Incorporation relief**

  This relief is available to those who transfer a business to a company in return for shares in the company. The effect of the relief is to delay paying CGT until the shares in the company are disposed of.
- **Gift hold-over relief**

  This relief is available where someone gives away business assets or sells them at an undervalue. The effect of the relief means that the person selling will not pay CGT or will pay a reduced amount. The person giving away the business asset and the person receiving it need to make a joint application for this relief.

15.11 Deduct annual exemption

The next stage of the calculation is to deduct the annual allowance which currently stands at £12,300.

15.12 Apply the relevant rate of tax

15.12.1 Higher-rate taxpayers

If the person making the gain is a higher-rate taxpayer, the following rates currently apply:

28% on residential property gains (this does not include the sale of a main residence).

20% on all other gains.

15.12.2 Basic-rate taxpayers

If the person is still within the basic-rate tax band when his capital gain minus the annual exemption is added to his taxable income, the rates are currently:

18% on residential property gains.
10% on all other gains.

Note that if any proportion of the sum is over the basic rate threshold it will be taxed at the higher rates:

28% on residential property gains (this does not include the sale of a main residence).
20% on all other gains.

15.13 Business property relief for inheritance tax

When a business owner dies and their assets pass to their personal representatives, this does not attract CGT but there may be inheritance tax (IT) implications. It may be possible to claim business property relief, which could either completely extinguish the IT liability or reduce it by 50%.

100% relief can be claimed on:

- A business or interest in a business.
- Shares in an unlisted company (shares not quoted on a recognised Stock Exchange).

50% relief can be claimed on:

- Shares in a listed company that gave the deceased control over the company immediately prior to the transfer.
- Land, buildings, or machinery owned by the deceased that was used, wholly or mainly, by the business which the deceased controlled or was a partner immediately prior to the transfer.
- Land, buildings, or machinery that was held on trust and the deceased was beneficially entitled to, that was used, wholly or mainly, by the business carried out by the deceased immediately before the transfer.

Chapter 15 revision points

- CGT is charged on gains made from a disposal of assets.
- Assets include any form of property but do not include the disposal of an individual's main residence.
- Disposal usually means sale, but it can mean a gift, swaps, and insurance pay-offs.
- CGT is usually not paid on gifts to spouses or charities.

16 Corporation tax and value-added tax

16.1 Chapter overview

This short chapter considers corporation tax and considers who is liable to pay it and how it is calculated. The chapter also outlines value-added tax (VAT).

16.2 Who pays corporation tax?

Corporation tax is paid by companies, and it also can be paid by unincorporated associations. Companies do not pay income tax and capital gains tax, although the main principles of corporation tax are largely derived from those discussed in previous chapters.

A company registered in the UK usually has to pay corporation tax on profits made in the UK and abroad.

16.3 How to calculate corporation tax

The steps to calculate corporation tax are essentially:

- Calculate income – this is predominantly trading income.
- Calculate chargeable gains – largely done on the same basis as capital gains tax; however, note that companies have fewer reliefs than individuals.
- Add the income and gains to find total income.
- Apply reliefs against total income. These reliefs are mainly available against trading losses.

16.4 Corporation tax rates

The corporation tax rate is currently 19%.

16.5 Value-added tax

VAT is referred to as a consumption tax or a goods and services tax, depending on which country you are in.

DOI: 10.4324/9781003289760-20

16.6 Who is liable to pay VAT?

The liability for paying VAT rests with any supplier required to be VAT registered who supplies goods or services and the liability arises at the time of delivery of the goods or service.

16.7 Rates of VAT

There are currently three rates of VAT: standard, reduced, and zero.

Standard rate	20%
Reduced rate	5%
Zero	0%

There are also a number of goods and services that are VAT exempt. Note that this is different from being charged VAT at zero per cent where businesses are able to claim back on certain expenditures. If a supply is VAT exempt, claiming back is not possible.

16.8 Requirement to be registered for VAT

A supplier is required to register for VAT if their annual taxable supplies exceed £85,000.

16.9 Responsibilities if VAT registered

If VAT registered, a supplier must charge VAT on every supply of goods or services. The supplier can also claim back for any VAT paid on goods and services. The supplier needs to complete a VAT return every three months. Annual and monthly schemes are also available.

16.10 Commercial awareness talking point

Understanding the different types of taxation is very useful to a newly qualified solicitor, particularly when advising clients on the use of individual business organisation types. It may be that the tax regime could be a good reason for choosing, or not choosing, a private limited company.

Chapter 16 revision points

- Companies are liable for corporation tax.
- Corporation tax is really a combination of income tax and capital gains tax but paid by companies.
- VAT is a consumption tax paid on goods and services that a company or business will need to pay if its annual taxable supplies are above £85,000.

PART 5 Insolvency

17 Corporate insolvency

17.1 Chapter overview

Insolvency is an important aspect of corporate law and solicitors commonly advise clients whose businesses are insolvent, or they are trading with other businesses who are. A working knowledge of the insolvency regime is important so that solicitors can offer advice both when insolvency has happened (or is imminent) and also so that businesses can prepare for the possibility of insolvency at a later date.

17.2 The impact of insolvency

A corporate insolvency can have a wide impact on a lot of stakeholders, both those operating within the business such as employees and also external stakeholders, principally creditors. Insolvency does not necessarily mean that the company will cease to exist, but it will most likely lead to an insolvency procedure. If the company is wound up (liquidated), this inevitably means that many creditors receive only a fraction of what they are owed.

17.3 The tests for insolvency

There are two tests for insolvency: the balance sheet test and the cash flow test.

The balance sheet test is when a court is satisfied that the value of a company's assets is less than the amount of its liabilities.

The cash flow test is when the court is satisfied that the company is unable to pay its debts as they become due.

A company is deemed insolvent (or unable to pay its debts) in the following circumstances:

- If the company fails to pay a statutory demand from a creditor for a debt of £750 or more within three weeks of the service of the demand at the company's registered office.

DOI: 10.4324/9781003289760-22

- If a creditor is awarded a judgment against the company and the company fails to pay when an enforcement procedure is attempted.

17.4 Insolvency options and procedures

There are a number of routes that the insolvent company can go down. These include:

- Liquidation.
- Administration.
- Fixed-asset receivership.
- Company voluntary arrangements (CVAs).

A new process that some companies can also take advantage of is the new (stand-alone) moratorium procedure.

17.5 Liquidation

Liquidation, or winding up, is essentially the death of the company. Winding up can happen in the following ways:

17.5.1 Members' voluntary winding up

This is a procedure open only to solvent companies. It requires the members to pass a special resolution for voluntary winding up (unless the articles contain a provision for an ordinary resolution). Before this resolution, the directors are required to make a statutory declaration of insolvency. A qualified insolvency practitioner is appointed as a liquidator.

17.5.2 Creditors' voluntary winding up

The creditors' voluntary winding up is initiated where members pass a winding-up resolution without the directors making a statutory declaration of solvency. Creditors have the right to nominate a liquidator if they do not approve the choice of the members. Creditors may also appoint a liquidation committee to act alongside the liquidator.

17.5.3 Winding up by the court

This is sometimes referred to as compulsory liquidation. The petition may be brought by the following (amongst others):

- The company.
- Directors.
- Any creditor or creditors.

In most circumstances it will be a creditor petitioning for the winding up using an unpaid statutory demand as evidence that the company is unable to pay its debts as they fall due.

The official receiver becomes the liquidator of the company if a winding up is ordered by the court. The official receiver can also seek nominations for an alternative liquidator from creditors and contributories.

17.5.4 Role of directors and appointment of a liquidator

To all intents and purposes, once a liquidator is appointed, the directors' role stops, and their powers are essentially transferred to the liquidator.

The liquidator has wide powers but is essentially charged with realising what assets the company has and distributing them amongst the creditors. The liquidator will also investigate and challenge past transactions of the company and the conduct of directors and in so doing add to the assets that can be distributed to creditors. The liquidator's powers to do this are sometimes referred to as claw-back provisions.

17.5.5 Claw-back provisions

The following are examples of claw-back of assets for creditors:

- Wrongful trading.
- Fraudulent trading.
- Transactions at an undervalue.
- Preferences.
- Setting aside a floating charge.

17.5.6 Wrongful trading

It is possible that a director of a company may be liable to contribute to the assets of a company on a winding up if there has been wrongful trading.

This will apply under the following circumstances:

- The company has gone into insolvent liquidation.
- Prior to the winding up the director knew, or ought to have known, that there was no reasonable prospect that the company would avoid going into insolvent liquidation.

The director has a defence if the court is satisfied that they took every step with a view to minimising the potential loss to the company's creditors that they ought to have done.

When deciding on liability, the courts use a statutory test that has a mixture of objective and subjective criteria:

> the facts which a director of a company ought to know or ascertain, the conclusions which he ought to reach and the steps which he ought to take are those which would be known or ascertained, or reached or taken, by a reasonably diligent person having both –

(a) the general knowledge, skill and experience that may reasonably be expected of a person carrying out the same functions as are carried out by that director in relation to the company, and
(b) the general knowledge, skill and experience that that director has.[1]

Although this test originated in the *Insolvency Act 1986* it has also been used in other legal contexts and is essentially now the same test used in the duty of care, skill, and diligence that was discussed in Chapter 8.

17.5.7 Fraudulent trading

Fraudulent trading occurs when the company's business has been "carried on with the intent to defraud creditors of the company, other creditors or for any fraudulent purpose".[2] The court can order anyone who was a knowing party to be liable to contribute to the company's assets.

Claims for fraudulent trading can be made by a liquidator or an administrator, and they are often made concurrently with claims for wrongful trading. Proving the necessary intention to defraud is very challenging, so success under wrongful trading claims is much more common.

If someone is liable for fraudulent trading, they may also face prosecution and a criminal conviction.

17.5.8 Transactions at an undervalue

Transactions at an undervalue are those transactions entered into by the company at a relevant time with a person and the company either receives no consideration or the value of the consideration received is significantly less than the value given by the company.

The "relevant time" is two years prior to the onset of insolvency. There is a rebuttable presumption of insolvency where the transaction is with a connected person.

The court will not make an order if it is satisfied:

(a) that the company which entered into the transaction did so in good faith and for the purpose of carrying on its business, and
(b) that at the time it did so there were reasonable grounds for believing that the transaction would benefit the company.[3]

The court has a wide discretion to make an order to restore the position to what it would have been had the transaction not taken place.

1 S.214 *Insolvency Act 1986*.
2 S.213 *Insolvency Act 1986*.
3 S.238(5) *Insolvency Act 1986*.

17.5.9 Preferences

A preference is where, at a relevant time, the company does something or allows something to be done that places a creditor in a better position than they would have been had the thing not been done.

The court will not make an order unless the company was influenced by a "desire"[4] to better the position of the creditor.

The relevant time is two years prior to the onset of insolvency where the transaction is with someone who is connected with the company (otherwise than by reason only of being its employee), otherwise the relevant time is six months prior to insolvency.

17.5.10 Setting aside a floating charge

If a company during the relevant time grants a floating charge and does not receive fresh consideration in exchange, then the charge will be void against the liquidator. The new consideration must be one of the following:

- Money paid, or goods or services supplied.
- The discharge or reduction of any debt of the company.
- Interest payable in relation to the above.

The relevant time is two years, ending with the presentation of the winding-up petition where the grantee of the charge is a connected person.

The relevant time is 12 months, ending with the presentation of the winding-up petition where the grantee of the charge is not a connected person.

17.5.11 Distribution of assets in a winding up

One of the fundamental principles of insolvency law is that of *pari passu*. This is the principle that assets are distributed to creditors in equal proportion to the amounts they are owed.

For example:

A petition is brought for the winding up of a company. After the expenses of winding up have been paid, the company has remaining assets of £50,000 but has liabilities to creditors for £100,000. The company has not granted any charges and there are no preferential creditors.

Creditor A is owed £10,000 by the insolvent company. If the principle of *pari passu* were strictly applied (ignoring all other rules of distribution), Creditor A would be

4 Re MC Bacon Limited [1990] BCLC 324.

entitled to 10% of the remaining assets because it is owed 10% of the overall liabilities of the company. Creditor A would receive £5,000.

In real life the scenario above is highly unlikely as there will normally be preferential creditors, secured creditors, and floating charge holders to consider.

In practice the order in which distribution of assets is made is:

- Secured creditors with a fixed charge.
  - This will usually be banks that have been granted a fixed charge over premises or fixed machinery.
- Liquidator fees and expenses.
- Preferential creditors.
  - This includes a certain amount for employees. A recent change to legislation means that HMRC is also a preferential creditor.
- Secured creditors with a floating charge.
  - This will usually be a bank with a floating charge over the undertaking.
- Unsecured creditors.
- Shareholders.

17.5.12 Top-slicing/ring fencing

The position of unsecured creditors has always been weak during a winding up as there is usually very little left over once the charge holders have been paid. To improve the position of unsecured creditors, there is now a mechanism whereby a proportion of the assets covered by a floating charge are distributed to unsecured creditors.

The amount capable of being ring fenced is:

- 50% of the first £10,000 of the net property that would otherwise be available to the floating charge holders.
- Then 20% up to a maximum of £800,000 for charges granted on or after 6 April 2020 (for charges created before that date the maximum is £600,000).

17.6 Administration

Although the administration process may end up with the same result as a liquidation, the starting premise is of corporate rescue which is demonstrated by the statutory objectives of administration which are set out in Schedule B of the *Insolvency Act 1986*:

(a) rescuing the company as a going concern, or
(b) achieving a better result for the company's creditors as a whole than would be likely if the company were wound up (without first being in administration), or

(c) realising property in order to make a distribution to one or more secured or preferential creditors.[5]

17.6.1 Appointing an administrator

The process begins with the appointment of an administrator who can be appointed by:

- An administration order of the court.
- The holder of a qualifying floating charge.
- The company or its directors.

17.6.2 Appointment by the court

The court may make an administration order only if it is satisfied of both of the following:

- The court is, or is likely to become, unable to pay its debts.
- The administration order is reasonably likely to achieve the purpose of administration.

17.6.3 Who can apply to court?

The following persons can apply to court for an administration order:

- The company.
- The directors of the company.
- One or more creditors of the company.
- The designated officer of a magistrates' court.

17.6.4 What can the court do?

After hearing the application for an administration order, the court has broad powers and can do the following things:

- Make the order.
- Dismiss the application.
- Adjourn the hearing.
- Make an interim order.
- Treat the application as a winding-petition.
- Make any other order the court sees fit.

17.6.5 Appointment by a holder of a qualifying floating charge

To be a qualifying floating charge, the debenture or other instrument that created the charge must either:

5 Paragraph 3, Schedule B1 *Insolvency Act 1986*.

- State that Paragraph 14 of Schedule B1 in the *Insolvency Act 1986* applies to the charge.
- Purport to empower the holder of the charge to appoint an administrator or,
- Purport to empower the holder of the charge to appoint an administrative receiver.

The qualifying charge holder must either:

- Hold a qualifying floating charge relating to the whole or substantially the whole of the company's property or,
- Hold a number of qualifying floating charges which taken together relate to the whole or substantially the whole of the company's property or,
- Hold charges and other forms of security that together with at least one qualifying floating charge relate to the whole or substantially the whole of the company's property.

17.6.6 Appointment by the company or the directors

A company or the directors may appoint an administrator. Schedule B of the *Insolvency Act 1986* states that an appointment can be made if any of the following apply:

- A petition for the winding up of the company has been presented and is not yet disposed of.
- An administration application has been made and is not yet disposed of.
- An administrative receiver of the company is in office.

Five days' notice of an intention to appoint an administrator must be given to qualifying floating charge holders. This notice is also filed at court with a statutory declaration that the company is unable to pay its debts or is likely to become unable to be able to pay its debts and is not in liquidation.

17.6.7 Moratorium

When a company goes into administration there is an automatic moratorium which means that creditors are unable to bring claims for debts owed for the duration of the administration period. There can also be an interim moratorium that comes into effect when the court receives the application.

17.6.8 Powers of the administrator

The administrator has wide powers and "may do anything necessary or expedient for the management of the affairs, business and property of the company."

17.6.9 The end of administration

The administration period is 12 months, but this can be extended, and often is, in complex cases. In some instances, the company can be rescued as a going concern and the directors can resume control of the company. The company can sometimes also exit administration by way of a company voluntary arrangement.

In many instances, the administration will end with the distribution of assets to creditors by the administrator or through the appointment of a liquidator.

17.7 Company voluntary arrangement

A company voluntary arrangement (CVA) is a court-sanctioned contractual agreement between creditors and the company whereby creditors agree to a reduction of their claims against the company and/or a scheme of arrangement for repayments.

This is a procedure that is designed to rescue a company. A CVA requires the agreement of 75% of creditors (by value of their claims) and at least 50% of unconnected creditors. It is possible that a CVA will bind creditors who are not in agreement. Rights of secured creditors and the priority of preferential creditors cannot be changed without the agreement of these creditors

17.7.1 When may a CVA be proposed?

A CVA is intended to be a cheap and flexible rescue procedure. It can be used in an attempt to stave off insolvency and therefore does not require evidence that the company is unable to pay its debts. Equally, the procedure is often used as a way to exit an administration.

17.7.2 Moratorium within a CVA

Unlike in an administration, a CVA does not normally include a moratorium. It is possible for small companies in a CVA to have a 28-day moratorium if they fulfil certain criteria. Occasionally CVAs are combined with an administration which comes with its own moratorium.

17.7.3 Proposing a CVA

Unless the company is in administration or in liquidation, a CVA proposal can only be made by directors of the company.

If the company is in administration or liquidation, only the administrator or the liquidator can make the proposal.

17.7.4 Appointment of a nominee

The CVA proposal involves the appointment of a nominee who must be a qualified insolvency practitioner. Where the company is in administration or liquidation this will often be the administrator or liquidator.

17.8 Fixed-asset receivership

One of the major advantages of holding a fixed charge over an insolvent company's assets is that the fixed-charge holder can appoint a receiver to sell the charged property or to receive rent from it. These are sometimes referred to as LPA receivers due to the powers in the *Law of Property Act 1925*; however, this is misleading as charge holders are more likely to use contractual powers from the loan agreement.

Creditors with floating charges that pre-date 15 September 2003 are able to appoint an administrative receiver – this is increasingly rare and in the vast majority of cases, floating charge holders must go down the administration route.

17.9 Moratorium (standalone procedure)

There is now an opportunity for directors of companies that either are insolvent or are likely to become insolvent to apply for a 20-working-day moratorium. This moratorium is intended as a short-term breathing space for a struggling company.

17.10 Commercial awareness talking point

Insolvency is a complex and detailed subject that is not always extensively taught on undergraduate law degrees. The subject is, however, inextricably linked with nearly every aspect of company law and business law and practice and should be at the forefront of a lawyer's mind when advising a client.

This is clearly the case when a business is in financial difficulty, but it is equally important at the beginning of the business, when deciding which type of business organisation to make and how to finance the business.

Understanding the dangers of insolvency for directors is vital, as is deciding on the appropriate type of insolvency procedure if one is needed.

Chapter 17 revision points

- There are two tests for insolvency; either:
  The balance sheet test, where a company's liabilities are greater than its assets,
  or
  The cash flow test, where a company is unable to pay its debts as they become due.
- The usual way for a creditor to prove a company is insolvent is to serve a statutory demand on a creditor for an unpaid debt – if this remains unpaid for 21 days, this is evidence that the company is insolvent.
- Insolvency does not mean that the company ceases to exist, but it may mean that the company enters into one of the following insolvency procedures:
  Company voluntary arrangement (CVA).

Administration.
Winding up.

- In a winding up, assets are distributed to creditors. Nominally this is according to the *pari passu* principle. In practice, secured creditors will receive more of their money than unsecured creditors.
- In an administration and a winding up, administrators and liquidators have the power to examine the affairs of the company and may seek to claw back money from directors and others.

18 Personal insolvency

18.1 Chapter overview

Personal insolvency, and in particular any subsequent bankruptcy, has historically been the cause of historical stigma. In modern times, more streamlined personal insolvency processes have been introduced that mean that in many cases personal insolvency, although not an ideal situation, does not have to be a permanent blight on an individual's life chances. Even with these changes, personal insolvency remains highly significant for solicitors, directors of companies, and partners and will often mean that the insolvent individual is unable to continue operating in business or practice in the same way for a period of time. An individual who is bankrupt cannot be a director of a company unless they have been granted permission by a court. Bankrupt individuals who continue as directors commit a criminal offence and can face two years' imprisonment and a fine.

18.2 Personal insolvency

An individual is insolvent when they are unable to pay their debts when they become due. Personal insolvency may lead to the individual being declared bankrupt; however, there are alternatives to bankruptcy which will be considered below.

18.3 Bankruptcy

Although often used synonymously with personal insolvency, bankruptcy is a process that an insolvent person may go into. The purpose of bankruptcy is to offer both debtor and creditor protection and has been defined in case law as follows:

> In the very broadest of terms, the purpose of bankruptcy is to provide protection to the bankrupt against the claims of creditors in respect of debts and liabilities as at the commencement of the bankruptcy and to realise the property owned by the bankrupt as at that date and distribute the realised proceeds among those creditors.[1]

1 *Azuonye v Kent* [2019] EWCA Civ 1289, per Lord Justice David Richards.

DOI: 10.4324/9781003289760-23

It could also be said that although bankruptcy is often a painful experience for a debtor, the process can also provide a much-needed escape from the financial chaos of personal insolvency.

18.4 Applying for bankruptcy – debtors

Individual debtors can make an online application to be made bankrupt. This is no longer a court process but involves an application to an adjudicator who will decide, usually within 28 days, whether the individual will be made bankrupt.

18.5 Petitioning for bankruptcy – creditors

A creditor can also initiate bankruptcy proceedings at the debtor's local county court if the following criteria can be met:

- The creditor must be owed at least £5,000 in liquidated unsecured debts. (A petition can still be brought if the creditor has a debt lower than £5,000 but the combined debts owed to other creditors also bringing proceedings amounts to or is greater than £5,000.)
- The creditor must prove that the debtor is insolvent. The debtor is deemed unable to pay his debts as they become due (therefore, insolvent) if the creditor serves a statutory demand on the debtor and the debtor neither complies with the demand nor takes action to set the demand aside within three weeks.
- The creditor needs to serve the bankruptcy petition on the debtor. This must be done in person usually by an agent who also needs to sign a witness statement confirming that they have served the petition. It is not uncommon for debtors to make themselves very elusive at this stage if they are keen to avoid bankruptcy. In these circumstances the creditor can apply to the court for an order permitting substituted service (such as posting the petition to the creditor's address).

18.6 The role of the official receiver/ trustee in bankruptcy

On bankruptcy, the assets of the debtor are vested in the official receiver who usually acts as the trustee in bankruptcy. The official receiver (OR) is a civil servant who is an officer of the court whose role is to administer the bankrupt person's estate and distribute assets to the bankrupt debtor's creditors. The OR is responsible for assessing the state of the debtors finances and has a number of powers to override certain transactions that the debtor has entered into in order to enhance and protect assets available for distribution. It is possible for the court to appoint an insolvency practitioner as trustee in bankruptcy other than the OR in some circumstances.

18.7 Property available for distribution

Most of the debtor's property (or former property as it is now vested in the OR) is available for distribution. The debtor will be permitted to keep some necessary assets for living, clothing, and furniture and tools of the trade for employment.

If the debtor is a homeowner, his title is vested in the OR on bankruptcy. If others have an interest or right to live in the home, eviction cannot happen without a court order and is likely to be very difficult for the first year after bankruptcy. After one year the creditor's interests are deemed to outweigh any others and an eviction order is much more common. A relatively recent addition to the law in this area is the "three-year rule" which means that if the OR does not sell the debtor's home in the three years after the bankruptcy order, then the property will return to the debtor.[2]

18.8 Challenging past transactions

The OR can challenge transactions that the debtor has entered into up to five years prior to the date of the bankruptcy order; however, a successful challenge is much more likely within two years because the OR would not need to prove insolvency.

Transactions that can be challenged include:

- **Unlawful preferences**

  This is broadly the same as an unlawful preference discussed in the corporate insolvency context (discussed in Chapter 17). A preference is where, at a relevant time, the bankrupt individual does something or allows something to be done that places a creditor in a better position than they would have been had the thing not been done.

  The relevant time is two years prior to the onset of insolvency where the transaction is with someone who is an associate of the individual (otherwise than by reason only of being its employee), otherwise the relevant time is six months prior to insolvency.
- **Transactions at an undervalue**

  Transactions at an undervalue are those transactions entered into by the bankrupt individual at a relevant time with another person and the bankrupt individual either receives no consideration, or the consideration is marriage or a civil partnership, or the value of the consideration received is significantly less than the value given by the company.

  The "relevant time" is five years prior to bankruptcy. If the transaction was more than two years prior to bankruptcy, then it must be proved that the

2 S.283A *Insolvency Act 1986.*

bankrupt individual was either insolvent at the time or became insolvent as a result of this transaction. Even if the transaction was over two years prior to bankruptcy, if the transaction was with an associate, then insolvency is presumed unless proven otherwise.

- **Transactions defrauding creditors**

  These are transactions at an undervalue that are specifically designed to prevent creditors having access to certain assets. In practice it is quite difficult to prove the necessary intention. The legal test comes from s.423 *Insolvency Act 1986*:

  > In the case of a person entering into such a transaction, an order shall only be made if the court is satisfied that it was entered into by him for the purpose –
  > (a) of putting assets beyond the reach of a person who is making, or may at some time make, a claim against him, or
  > (b) of otherwise prejudicing the interests of such a person in relation to the claim which he is making or may make.

  If the court finds there is an infringement, it has a wide discretion to make an order aimed at putting the creditor in a position they would have been in had the transaction not been entered into and otherwise protect the interests of those who are the victims of the transaction.

- **Extortionate credit transactions**

  The trustee in bankruptcy has the power to apply to court to adjust a credit transaction entered into under three years prior to bankruptcy if the terms of the agreement are grossly exorbitant. This power seems to be used very rarely and there is no reported case law about it.

18.9 Distribution of assets

The distribution of assets to creditors follows similar principles to corporate insolvency with *pari passu* applying, with the general presumption that all creditors rank equally, and they are entitled to receive a share of the debtor's assets proportionate to how much they are owed of the total debts. In practice, as with corporate insolvency, *pari passu* is rarely the case because some creditors have secured interests. If there are fixed creditors, for example a lender who has been granted a mortgage on a property, the lender can sell the charged property (subject to a court order considering rights or interests of others in the property).

Remaining assets will be distributed in the following order:

- Bankruptcy costs. Principally the professional charges of the OR.
- Preferential creditors. Any employees and also HMRC.
- Unsecured creditors.
- Postponed creditors. This refers to debts owed to a spouse or civil partner of the debtor.

18.10 Discharge from bankruptcy

Bankruptcy begins when the order is made and ends when the bankrupt individual is discharged. This is nominally on the one-year anniversary of the bankruptcy order but in practice this can be a lot longer.

18.11 Bankruptcy alternatives

Although bankruptcy may be unavoidable it is normal for debtors and creditors to consider various options first.

18.11.1 Informal negotiation

The obvious thing for an insolvent debtor to do is to enter into individual agreements with creditors. It is often in the interests of a creditor to accept compromise payments or to make extensions on loan payments. Such negotiations can be very useful, if only to ascertain whether the debtor's position is merely temporarily difficult or more terminal.

18.11.2 Individual voluntary arrangement (IVA)

An individual voluntary arrangement (IVA) is very similar to a company voluntary arrangement (CVA) discussed in the previous chapter. IVAs are sought after a bankruptcy petition has been served or to avoid one completely.

The effect of an IVA is to avoid some of the stigma and restrictions that come with bankruptcy. The IVA can give a much-needed breathing space because it will prevent creditors bringing actions to enforce debts. The IVA needs the agreement of 75% of unsecured creditors who will be contacted by the nominated insolvency practitioner.

An IVA sometimes leads to bankruptcy anyway as the insolvency practitioner can make the debtor bankrupt and/or cancel the IVA if the debtor fails to make agreed payments.

18.11.3 Debt relief order

In certain circumstances a debtor can apply for a debt relief order (DRO) which will bring protection from creditors for a number of debts. The following criteria need to apply:

- The debtor owes £30,000 or less.
- The debtor has £75 or less available income each month.
- The debtor does not own their own house.
- The debtor does not have assets worth £2,000 or more.
- The debtor does not own a car worth more than £2,000.
- The debtor has not applied for a DRO in the last six years.

18.12 Commercial awareness talking point

Although much of the stigma of bankruptcy has been diminished in recent years and the processes have been significantly improved, personal insolvency is extremely stressful and can often present problems that can appear insurmountable to individuals. Clients need to be drawn to the range of options that are available and may even mean that bankruptcy is not inevitable.

Chapter 18 revision points

- Personal insolvency occurs when an individual is unable to pay their debts as they fall due; this will usually be determined by the non-payment of a statutory demand or the non-payment of a court order.
- Personal insolvency can lead to bankruptcy and a creditor can petition to court if the debt is £5,000 or more.
- Debtors can also apply for bankruptcy through an online, out-of-court process.
- Bankruptcy is less stigmatised than previously and usually lasts just a year.
- Bankruptcy gives a debtor protection and ensures distribution of available assets to creditors.
- On bankruptcy, the debtor's assets are vested in the trustee in bankruptcy (usually the official receiver) This includes the family home; however, third parties with rights and interests have a certain amount of protection from eviction for 12 months.
- There are alternatives to bankruptcy that should be explored first in most situations: negotiation with creditors, individual voluntary arrangements, and debt relief orders.

PART

6 Practice questions

19 Multiple-choice questions

19.1 Chapter overview

The following multiple-choice questions are designed to reflect the content of many of the areas discussed in previous chapters. The design of the questions is based on the style of the sample questions provided by the SRA for SQE1.

19.2 Business organisations

1. A client runs a small travel agent business. She specialises in organising adventure holidays in the UK and abroad. The client is currently a sole trader, but she is considering going into business with a friend and is seeking advice on which business form to use. The client is very organised and happy to do additional administration. The client hopes that formalising the business may make it more attractive to her international clients. She wants the business to grow but is concerned about any exposure she may have to personal liability if the business should fail.

Which of the following is the best advice to give the client on potential business forms?

A. The client should form an ordinary partnership with her friend as this would be the most cost-effective option.
B. The client should incorporate a private limited company because it will offer her limited liability and could help the business raise capital.
C. The client should incorporate a limited liability partnership because it will offer her limited liability and means she does not have to file tax accounts.
D. The client should form an ordinary partnership because its separate legal personality will be useful when signing contracts.
E. The client should form a limited company because this is invariably better for tax reasons.

DOI: 10.4324/9781003289760-25

2. A client is considering buying ordinary shares in a private limited company run by two of his friends. The company's articles are in the form of the model articles. The client is already very busy with several different projects so he would like some advice on the extent of his potential new role within the company and how he might benefit financially from it.

Which of the following best describes the position of a shareholder in a private limited company?

A. Shareholders are salaried employees responsible for the day-to-day running of the company and make most decisions of the company.
B. Shareholders are not involved in the day-to-day running of the company and are only required to take a few important decisions. If the company makes a profit, they may be awarded dividend payments.
C. Shareholders owe fiduciary duties to the company and are required to promote the company's success. If the company makes a profit, they may be awarded dividend payments.
D. Shareholders are not involved in the day-to-day running of the company and do not have any influence on the decision-making in the company. If the company makes a profit, they may be awarded dividend payments.
E. Shareholders receive salaries and advise directors on important decisions of the company.

19.3 Formation of the company

3. A client is considering operating his business through a private limited company. He understands that limited liability may offer some protection to him but is a little vague about the concept. He is thinking of being the only shareholder and director in the company. He will incorporate a company using the model articles.

Which of the following explains the client's limited liability in a private company best?

A. His liability will be limited to the nominal value of his paid-up shares. This means that it is unlikely that he will be sued for any debts of the company if the business fails.
B. His liability will be limited to the nominal value of his paid-up shares. This means that it is impossible for him to be sued for any debts of the company if the business fails.
C. Limited liability means that the company is protected from having to pay creditors.

D. The client's liability for the debts of the company is unlimited.
E. In a private limited company, a director's liability is limited by insurance.

4. A client is seeking to bring a personal injury claim for negligence against a chemicals company that employed him. The client inhaled chemicals that were incorrectly labelled and he was not given protective equipment. He has heard that the company has gone into liquidation, and he wants to know if it is possible to sue the company's parent company who set out the health and safety policies for all its subsidiary companies.

Can the client bring a claim against the parent company?

A. Yes, because the parent and subsidiary company are a single economic unit.
B. No. The client was not employed by the parent company.
C. Yes. He can claim against the parent as the subsidiary is clearly acting as its agent.
D. Possibly. The parent company may owe a duty of care to employees of the subsidiary.
E. Possibly. The court may find that the corporate veil can be pierced in the interests of justice.

5. An IT specialist is the sole director and shareholder in a private limited company that was incorporated in September 2018. The company adopted the model articles. In August 2018, immediately prior to incorporation, the IT specialist saw an opportunity to purchase £20,000 of computer hardware on behalf of the company from a major supplier. As the hardware has been defective, the IT specialist and the company have so far refused to pay the £20,000 and the supplier is bringing legal proceedings for the debt.

Which of the below best explains who is potentially liable for the debt?

A. The company, because it is a separate legal personality, and the specialist made the contract on its behalf.
B. The specialist, because the company was not in existence when the contract was formed, and the specialist was purporting to act on the company's behalf.
C. The company because the specialist was acting as the company's agent.
D. The company and the specialist are jointly liable.
E. The company only, as its articles permit pre-incorporation contracts.

6. A client has decided to incorporate a private limited company to run a business selling computer software. The company was successfully registered

in September 2020. The client specialist is the only director and shareholder. In August 2020, the client formed a contract on behalf of the new company with a large multinational firm to purchase computer hardware. The multinational firm was unaware that the company had not yet been incorporated. The computer hardware was delivered in October 2020, but the client claims that it is defective. So far, the bill for the hardware is unpaid and the multinational firm is about to commence legal proceedings to recover the debt.

Can the client be sued on the contract for the computer hardware?

A. No, because he was acting for the company when he formed the contract.
B. Yes, because the client was purporting to act on behalf of the company or as its agent and there was no evidence of a contrary intention.
C. Yes, because as an agent for the company, the client was personally liable for the debt.
D. No, as the hardware was delivered after the company was registered, it will be the company that is liable.
E. No, because the multinational firm should have done a company search as due diligence before entering the contract.

19.4 Constitution of the company

7. A client runs a partnership with two friends. They have decided to incorporate a private limited company. The client has heard that the articles of association are a statutory contract and would like advice on how they can protect her rights in the company.

What explains best how rights in the articles can be enforced by shareholders?

A. The articles are a statutory contract that bind the shareholders and the company. All rights in the articles can be enforced by shareholders.
B. The articles are a statutory contract that bind the shareholders and the company. The rights in the articles can only be enforced by the company as it is a separate legal entity.
C. The articles are a statutory contract that bind the shareholders and the company. Shareholders can enforce rights that relate to their shares, for example, voting rights.
D. The articles are a statutory contract that bind the shareholders and the company. Rights in the articles can only be enforced through a derivative action.
E. The articles are a statutory contract that binds the shareholders and the company. Only rights relating to the management of the company can be enforced. For example, the right to be a director.

8. A client runs a partnership with two friends. They have decided to incorporate a private limited company. The client has heard about shareholders' agreements and would like to know in what ways they can protect her interests.

Which best explains the nature and purpose of a shareholders' agreement?

A. A shareholders' agreement is a contract between some or all the shareholders. It is a private agreement to which the company is not party. These agreements can protect minority shareholders' interests and are often easier to enforce than the articles.
B. A shareholders' agreement is a company document registered at Companies House on incorporation. It can be enforced in certain situations by individual shareholders if their rights have been infringed.
C. A shareholders' agreement is a contract between all the shareholders, past and present, in the company. It can be amended by special resolution.
D. A shareholders' agreement is a contractual agreement like the articles of association. Companies can either have articles of association, a shareholders' agreement, or both.
E. A shareholders' agreement is a contract between the shareholders that is required by law to be filed at Companies House. The agreement contains rules for the governance of the company that can be enforced by shareholders.

9. A private limited company was incorporated in 2016 with the model articles (unamended). There are two directors. The company would like to form a new contract with a new supplier that is managed and owned by one of the director's spouses. The director has declared his interest in the transaction.

What needs to happen so that the board can resolve to enter into the contract?

A. The shareholders must pass a special resolution to disapply Model Article 14.
B. The shareholders must pass an ordinary resolution to disapply Model Article 14.
C. The shareholders must pass an ordinary resolution to remove Model Article 14.
D. No shareholder action is required as the board can enter into the contract under its powers of general management.
E. No shareholder action is required as the director has already declared his interest in the proposed transaction.

19.5 Roles in the company

10. The board of a private limited company would like to remove its company secretary. The company secretary is not a director of the company but does hold 30% of the issued ordinary shares. It is likely that the company secretary will resist removal. The company was incorporated in 2018 with the model articles.

What procedures need to be followed to remove the company secretary?

A. An ordinary resolution at a general meeting is required and special notice is required. Companies House must also be notified.
B. A special resolution at a general meeting is required and special notice is required.
C. An ordinary resolution is required; this can be a written resolution or be done at a general meeting. Companies House must also be notified.
D. A board resolution is required, and the company must notify Companies House.
E. A special resolution is required at a general meeting or by written resolution.

19.6 Financing the company

11. A client is a director and shareholder in a private limited company in which she holds £75,000 out of the £100,000 of issued share capital. The share capital consists of only one class of ordinary shares. There is one other director who holds the remaining 25% of shares. The business has prospered and now has significant assets including expensive heavy machinery valued at over £200,000. The two directors have not always agreed, however, and there have been occasions when the client has had to rely on her majority voting power to ensure that important decisions went in her favour. Both directors are agreed that the company needs to raise capital for expansion. Neither director wants to take on any personal liability. The other director has suggested that the company issues £100,000 in ordinary shares to her husband. Your client is uncertain about whether the company should do this or simply take a loan from the bank.

Which of the following would be the best advice to the client in this case?

A. Issue shares to the director's husband because a loan would not be possible because the company would be unable to grant the bank any security.

B. A loan, secured by a fixed charge on the machinery, may well be the best option.
C. Issuing ordinary shares to the other director's husband is the best option as they have worked well in the past.
D. A loan would be the best option, but one or both directors would need to offer a personal guarantee to the bank.
E. Issuing ordinary shares to the other directors would be the best option as this will mean that in the future the client will be entitled to a larger share of the profits.

12. The directors of a private limited company are seeking new investment and would like to allot 10,000 new ordinary shares to new shareholders. The company was registered in 2012 and adopted the model articles which are unamended. There is only one class of shares.

Is shareholder approval required for the new allotment of shares to go ahead?

A. Yes, because although the board have the power to allot shares, a special resolution is required to disapply the existing shareholders' pre-emption rights.
B. No, because under their powers of general management, the board always has an unrestricted power to allot shares.
C. No, because it is a private company with only one class of shares and the board already has authority.
D. Yes, shareholder approval is always required for an allotment of shares.
E. No, because the shares are ordinary shares and do not attract class rights.

13. The board of a private limited company would like to make an allotment of shares to a new investor. The company was incorporated in 2015 with the model articles (unamended) and there is only one class of shares. The new investor's investment is conditional on him having a 25% share in the company. To achieve this, the company needs to disapply the pre-emption rights of the other shareholders. This is likely to be resisted by one of the existing shareholders who holds 30% of the shares.

If the shareholder opposes the disapplication, can it go ahead?

A. No. A special resolution is required, and the 30% shareholder will be able to prevent this.
B. Yes. The remaining shareholders will have enough votes for the ordinary resolution required.
C. Yes. The board has the power in the articles to disapply the pre-emption rights.

D. No. The disapplication would be a breach of the directors' duty to exercise care, skill, and diligence.
E. No. The allotment can only go ahead if the shareholders waive their pre-emption rights by deed.

19.7 Shareholders' decision-making

14. A client is one of three directors of a private limited company. The client has been advised by his accountant that it would be tax efficient if he took a loan from the company of £20,000. The two other directors are in favour of the loan. The client holds exactly 50% of the issued ordinary shares in the company. The company was incorporated in 2014 and the articles are in the form of the model articles which have not been amended.

Does the loan require shareholder approval?

A. Yes, an ordinary resolution is required.
B. Yes, a special resolution is required because all directors have a conflict of interest.
C. The loan can only be made with a court order.
D. No, the loan can be approved by the board using their powers of general management in the articles.
E. No, shareholder approval is not required because the client holds sufficient shares to get an ordinary resolution.

15. A private limited company was incorporated in 2010 with the model articles. There is only one class of shares and there is an issued share capital of 100,000 ordinary shares which have a nominal value of £2 each. All of the shares are paid up. A client is a shareholder in the company and would like the company to call a general meeting to discuss a number of issues that are concerning him about how the company is being run. The client holds 3,000 shares.

Can the client require the board to call a general meeting?

A. Yes, any shareholder has the right to call a general meeting.
B. No, because he holds less than 5% of the issued ordinary shares.
C. Yes, because he holds over 10% of the issued share capital.
D. No, the power to call a general meeting is vested in the board of directors only.

E. No, the model articles stipulate that only shareholders with 25% of the issued shares can call general meetings.

19.8 Directors' decision-making

16. The board of a private limited company would like to remove its company secretary. The company secretary is not a director of the company but does hold 30% of the issued ordinary shares. It is likely that the company secretary will resist removal.

What procedures need to be followed to remove the company secretary?

A. An ordinary resolution at a general meeting is required and special notice is required. Companies House must also be notified.
B. A special resolution at a general meeting is required and special notice is required.
C. An ordinary resolution is required; this can be a written resolution or at a general meeting. Companies House must also be notified.
D. A board resolution is required, and the company must notify Companies House.
E. A special resolution is required at a general meeting or by written resolution.

17. The board of a private limited company are meeting to discuss entering into a contract. A client is one of the directors and he has declared an interest in the proposed transaction. The company was registered in 2010 and the articles are in the form of the model articles (unamended). There are three directors on the board.

What quorum and voting requirements need to be fulfilled for the board to pass a resolution to enter the contract?

A. The required quorum is two directors. The client can vote and be counted in the quorum because he has declared his interest in the transaction. A bare majority of directors in favour is required.
B. The required quorum is two directors. The client cannot vote but can be counted in the quorum because he has declared his interest in the transaction. Two of the directors must be in favour for the resolution to pass.
C. The required quorum is three directors. To proceed, the shareholders must first pass an ordinary resolution to disapply a regulation in the articles that prevents the client voting or being counted in the quorum.

D. The required quorum is two directors. The client cannot vote or be counted in the quorum unless an ordinary resolution is passed to disapply a provision of the model articles. Without this disapplication the other directors must both approve for the resolution to pass.
E. The required quorum is three directors. The client can count in the quorum but must not vote.

19.9 Directors' duties

18. A private limited company was incorporated in 2010 with the model articles with one amendment that excludes all pre-emption rights. There are three directors who between them own 40% of the voting shares. One shareholder owns 50% of the shares and the board are quite concerned that this amount of voting power may cause the board problems in the future. The directors have decided that they would like to make a fresh allotment of shares to another shareholder to distribute voting power more evenly. The directors are not motivated by personal profit but are concerned about the future of the company.

Is there a danger that the board could breach their directors' duties by allotting the new shares?

A. No, the board are behaving honestly and are seeking to promote the success of the company.
B. No, because the articles exclude the statutory pre-emption rights, the board has the power to allot the shares.
C. Yes, there is a possibility that a court may find that, even though they have acted honestly, the directors have not exercised their powers for a proper purpose.
D. Yes, the directors are in breach of their duty to promote the success of the company.
E. Yes, the directors have breached their duty to avoid conflicts of interest.

19. A client is one of three directors of a small engineering company. He also owns 40% of the shares in a manufacturing company. His fellow directors do not know about his shareholding. The engineering company is negotiating a large contract with the manufacturing company to supply engineering services.

Advise the client what steps, if any, he needs to take in order that he does not breach his directors' duties.

A. The client will not be in breach of duty providing that he honestly believes that the contract is in the company's best interest.

B. The client needs to disclose an interest in a proposed transaction with the company. He can make this declaration to the board.
C. The client is in breach of his duty to avoid conflicts of interest. He needs to ask the board to ratify his breach.
D. The client needs to disclose his interest in the engineering company. The disclosure must be made at a general meeting.
E. The client does not need to declare an interest because there is no reasonable possibility of a conflict of interest.

20. A client is one of five directors of a private limited company. The company's articles are in the form of the model articles. The client joined the company two months ago and had to miss a board meeting recently due to illness. He has just discovered that the company has signed a lucrative contract with a large company in which the client holds about 30% of the shares. The other board members are unaware of this holding.

What steps does the client need to take to avoid liability for breach of duty?

A. No action is required, because the contract was made without his knowledge so there is no reasonable possibility of a conflict.
B. The client is in breach of his duty to avoid conflicts of interest; he will need to ask the shareholders to ratify the breach with an ordinary resolution.
C. The client should declare the nature and extent of his interest to the other directors as soon as is reasonably practicable.
D. The client has failed to declare an interest in a proposed transaction with the company; he will need to ask the shareholders to ratify the breach with an ordinary resolution.
E. The client should declare the nature and extent of his interest to the shareholders as soon as is reasonably practicable.

21. A director of a private limited company is in breach of his directors' duty to avoid conflicts of interest. A minority shareholder would like advice on the situation and is considering legal action. The company is solvent.

Who can sue the director for the breach of duty?

A. Only the company can sue, as the duties are owed to the company. It will be for the board to decide whether to bring an action for breach.
B. Only the shareholders can instigate an action through an ordinary resolution at a general meeting.
C. The company can bring an action for breach. It will be for the board to decide whether to bring an action for breach. Individual shareholders may also be able to bring an unfair prejudice petition or instigate a derivative action.

D. Only the company can sue, as the duties are owed to the company. It will be for the shareholders to approve by special resolution.
E. Individual shareholders only, by bringing a derivative action on behalf of the company.

22. A director of a private limited company has accidentally breached his duty to avoid conflicts of interest. The company has not suffered a loss from the breach and the rest of the board are hoping that the breach can be ratified. Although some shareholders are opposed, 60% of the shareholders who are entitled to vote on the ratification are happy to support the board. The company was incorporated in 2014 with the model articles. There is only one class of issued share capital.

Is it likely that the breach will be ratified?

A. Yes. The breach can be ratified by a board resolution.
B. No. The breach can only be ratified by special resolution of the shareholders.
C. Yes. The breach can be ratified by an ordinary resolution of the shareholders.
D. No. The breach cannot be ratified.
E. No. The breach cannot be ratified by the company. It can only be forgiven by a court as a minor breach.

23. A client is a director of a private limited company that was incorporated in 2014. On incorporation, the company adopted the model articles with one amendment stating that contracts made by directors over £50,000 needed to be authorised by the board.

The client saw a good business opportunity and entered a contract for £60,000 with another firm. The board has now refused to authorise the contract and has informed the firm that the company is not bound by the contract.

Can the company still be bound by the contract?

A. No, because the contract was beyond the powers of the director who was acting outside the company's constitution. The contract is void.
B. No, because the firm had constructive notice of the clause in the company's articles.
C. Yes. The client is in breach of his duty, but the company can still be bound.
D. Yes. The client is not in breach of his duty as he has acted honestly to pursue a genuine opportunity for the company.
E. No. If a director is in breach of his duty, he cannot bind the company.

19.10 Transactions with directors requiring shareholder approval

24. A private limited company was incorporated in 2010 and adopted the model articles which have not been amended. Having operated profitably for the past ten years the company is now looking to expand and the board are considering buying some expensive new machinery, independently valued at £95,000, from the spouse of one of the directors. According to its most recent set of accounts, the company's net profits were £1,100,000 and it had net assets of £900,000. All directors are in favour of purchasing the machinery.

Does the purchase require shareholder approval?

A. No, because the value of the machinery is less than 10% of the net profits of the company.
B. Yes, because the value of the machinery is greater than 10% of the net assets of the company.
C. Yes, because a transaction with a director's spouse always needs to be approved by a general meeting.
D. Yes, this will need to be approved by special resolution in a general meeting.
E. No, because the purchase is of machinery and not land.

25. The directors of a private limited company have decided to sell some heavy machinery to the spouse of one of the directors. According to the most recent accounts the machinery is valued at £105,000. The company has net profits of £800,000 and net assets of £2,000,000.

The company was incorporated in 2018 with the model articles which have not been amended.

Does the sale of machinery require shareholder approval?

A. Yes, because the transaction involves the sale and purchase of a non-cash asset whose value exceeds 10% of the company's net profits.
B. Yes, because the transaction involves the sale of a non-cash asset whose value exceeds £100,000.
C. No, because although there is a potential conflict of interest, this can be disclosed to the board.
D. Yes, because all potential conflicts of interest should be declared at a general meeting.
E. No, because the value of the non-cash asset does not exceed 10% of the company's net assets.

26. A client is one of three directors of a private limited company. The client has been advised by his accountant that it would be tax efficient if he took a loan from the company of £20,000. The two other directors are in favour of the loan. The client holds exactly 50% of the issued ordinary shares in the company. The company was incorporated in 2014 and the articles are in the form of the model articles which have not been amended.

Does the loan require shareholder approval?

A. Yes, an ordinary resolution is required.
B. Yes, a special resolution is required because all directors have a conflict of interest.
C. No, the loan can only be made with a court order.
D. No, the loan can be approved by the board using the powers of general management in the articles.
E. No, shareholder approval is not required because the client holds sufficient shares to get an ordinary resolution.

27. The board of a private limited company want to employ a new director on a five-year contract to lead them in an exciting new development. The proposed contract contains a term under which the company can terminate the contract with three months' notice. The company was incorporated in 2012 under the model articles which have not been amended.

Do the appointment and the contract require shareholder approval?

A. No. The board have the power to appoint the director under the articles. The contract does not need to be approved by the shareholders because the contract can be terminated with less than two years' notice.
B. Yes. The appointment requires approval by ordinary resolution and the proposed contract needs a special resolution as it is for longer than two years.
C. The board has the power to appoint the director under the articles. The shareholders need to approve the contract by ordinary resolution.
D. No. The board always has the power to appoint a director and to approve the contract.
E. Yes. The appointment of the director and the contract both need ordinary resolutions.

28. A director of a private limited company has agreed to resign his position with the company. The board have agreed to pay him £1,000 as compensation for loss of office. The company was incorporated in 2010 with the model articles (unamended).

Is shareholder approval required for the payment?

A. Yes. An ordinary resolution is required. This can either be a written resolution or in a general meeting.
B. No. The payment is a small payment; therefore it is exempt from the requirement for shareholder approval.
C. No. The model articles contain a provision exempting the requirement for private limited companies.
D. Yes. A special resolution is required.
E. Yes. The payment must be authorised by an ordinary resolution at a general meeting.

19.11 Minority shareholder protection

29. A client is the director of a private limited company that has been involved in a dispute with a minority shareholder that has led to the filing of an unfair prejudice petition. The shareholder holds 20% of the issued ordinary shares. Although all shareholders in the company were once very good friends, their relationship has now broken down irreconcilably. The client is concerned that the shareholder will win the petition and is concerned about what the remedy imposed by the court might be. The company is very profitable and relations between all other shareholders and directors are excellent.

Which of the following is the most likely remedy to be ordered by the court if there is a finding of unfair prejudice?

A. An order that the minority shareholder's shares are purchased by the company or the other shareholders.
B. An order that the minority shareholder purchases the shares of the majority.
C. An order that the minority shareholding is transferred to a third party.
D. An order that makes the minority shareholder a director of the company.
E. An order for a just and equitable winding up of the company.

19.12 Partnerships

30. A client has decided to incorporate an LLP with three business partners to run a new enterprise. Two of the business partners are keen to invest in the partnership but do not wish to be involved in the management at all. They are keen on your client being one of the designated partners.

Which of the following best describes the position of a designated partner?

A. Designated members are legally qualified solicitors or accountants who fulfil the same role company secretaries perform in public listed companies.
B. Designated members take responsibility for the management of the partnership and have unlimited liability for the debts of the partnership.
C. Designated members have more duties than ordinary members and these involve the responsibility to file documents with Companies House.
D. Designated members are nominated by Companies House.
E. Designated members are qualified chartered accountants.

31. A client has been in an ordinary partnership with two friends for the past two years. During that time the three partners have contributed equally to the capital of the business. In accordance with the partnership agreement, the client has received half of the profits; the remaining half has been divided equally between the other partners.

The business has recently suffered large losses and is being pursued by creditors.

What advice should the client receive about her potential liability for debts of the business?

A. The client could be sued for all the debts because in an ordinary partnership, partners are jointly and severally liable for the debts of the partnership.
B. The client is only liable for half of the debts because in an ordinary partnership, partners are jointly liable for the debts of the partnership.
C. The client is not liable for the debts because the partnership is a separate legal personality independent of the partners.
D. The client is only liable for one-third of the debts of the partnership.
E. The client's liability is limited to the paid-up value of her initial investment in the partnership.

32. A client was one of three partners in a partnership from 2015 until she left in July 2020, selling her partnership share to a new partner. There is no partnership agreement and the partnership had not been registered at Companies House. Litigation has just been commenced by a supplier who is claiming that the partnership is liable for £20,000 for an unpaid debt relating to a contract that was formed between the partnership and the supplier in August 2020.

Which of the following is the best explanation of the client's potential liability for the £20,000 debt?

A. The client cannot be liable because she was not in the partnership when the contract with the supplier was formed.
B. The client will not be liable for the debt providing the notice requirements under the Partnership Act have been complied with and she has not held herself out (or allowed herself to be held out) as being a partner since retiring.
C. Partners are jointly and severally responsible for all partnership debts, the client will always be liable unless the partnership is dissolved.
D. The client will not be liable, and neither will the partners, because the partnership is a limited liability partnership and has separate legal personality.
E. The client will always be jointly liable for her share of the debt with the new partner.

33. A client is in an ordinary partnership with her two nephews. They do not have a written partnership agreement. The client contributed 50% to the start-up capital of the partnership and the nephews 25% each. The client has become irritated that she has been working full time for the partnership and the nephews have been barely working one day per week. The partners have all agreed to dissolve the partnership and go their separate ways. There are no creditors.

Which of the following best describes how the partnership income and capital profits may be distributed?

A. The partners will share the capital profits equally, but the client will get more of the income profits because she has worked more hours.
B. The client will receive 50% of all profits.
C. As there is no partnership agreement, the presumption is that all profits will be shared equally.
D. The nephews are in breach of their fiduciary duties in not working full time and are not entitled to any profits.
E. The partners will share the capital profits equally, but the client is entitled to 50% of the income profits.

34. Four IT specialists run a business as an ordinary partnership. Three of the partners would like to make an amendment to the partnership agreement so that profits can be shared according to how much time each partner spends in the business. The partnership agreement is very short and contains no provisions relating to decision-making or changing the agreement.

Advise the partners if they can change the partnership agreement if the fourth partner does not support the change?

A. No. The partnership agreement can only be altered by all partners agreeing.
B. Yes. The agreement can be altered by 75% of the partners.
C. Yes. The agreement can be altered by a bare majority of the partners.
D. Yes. Agreements relating to profit sharing can be altered by a bare majority.
E. No. All partnership decisions must be unanimous.

35. Four partners have been running a small market bakery stall for the past three years. The partnership has not been registered at Companies House. Recently three of the partners have decided that they can no longer work with the fourth partner for largely personal reasons that do not relate to the partnership business. The written partnership agreement does not contain any clauses relating to the removal of a partner.

What advice should the three partners be given on their power to remove a partner?

A. As there is nothing to the contrary in the partnership agreement, the fourth partner can be removed by the other partners as they are in the majority.
B. As the partnership agreement does not contain a clause for the removal of a director, the three partners cannot remove the other partner.
C. The fourth partner can be removed because the other partners agree and together constitute 75% of the partners.
D. The fourth partner can be removed if two other partners agree.
E. The fourth partner can be removed by the other partners if they have contributed over 50% of the partnership capital.

36. A client is one of three partners in a pottery-making business. The partnership has not been registered at Companies House and there is no written partnership agreement. The two other partners are very keen that the business expand and would like to employ a new marketing director whose role would be to find new markets for existing products made by the partnership The client is not convinced by this plan and thinks that expanding is not a good idea in the current economic climate.

Advise the client if the decision to employ the marketing director needs his approval.

A. The decision to employ the marketing director requires unanimous consent of the partners because it is a significant change to the business.

B. The decision to employ the marketing director can be made by a majority of the partners as it does not change the nature of the business.
C. Decisions to employ staff can only be made by unanimous consent of the partners.
D. Decisions to employ staff can only be made by 75% of the partners.
E. The marketing director cannot be employed because ordinary partnerships do not have legal personality.

19.13 Business accounts and tax

37. A company has a pool of plant and equipment worth £2,370,500 at the start of the period. There were additions of £550,000 during the current period.

If nothing else has changed, what would be the capital allowance for the current period?

A. £426,690.
B. £550,000.
C. £976,690.
D. £525,690.
E. £1,000,000.

38. A company has a pool of plant and equipment worth £2,370,500 at the start of the period. There were additions of £550,000 during the current period.

What would be the WDV of this pool of assets to be carried forward to the next financial period?

A. £1,943,810.
B. £1,820,500.
C. £1,000,000.
D. £426,690.
E. £550,000.

39. A business provides the following information which relates to the previous accounting period:

Income and expenditure items	£
Wages and salaries	602,000
Sale of plant and equipment	200,000
Rent and insurance of buildings	45,000
Materials used in the production of goods	200,500
Power, light, heat, and water used	78,000
Sales to good and services customers	1,645,000

What is the trading profit for tax purposes for this entity for the accounting period?

A. £997,500.
B. £797,500.
C. £1,645,000.
D. £919,500.
E. £719,500.

40. A sole trader is concerned that HMRC may decide that some of his recent tax arrangements may have contravened the general anti-abuse rule (GAAR).

If there has been an infringement which of the following is correct?

A. HMRC will bring a criminal prosecution for breach of the GAAR.
B. HMRC will impose a fine for breach of the GAAR.
C. HMRC will require the sole trader to make an adjusted payment of tax.
D. HMRC will refer the matter to the Serious Fraud Office.
E. HMRC will give the sole trader a written warning as it is a first offence.

41. In the 2022/2023 tax year a man has received the following payments:

Gross salary from employment: £12,250.
Interest on savings: £4,999.
Dividends from shares: £2,000.

He also made a profit of £10,000 on a one-off sale of a vintage car he purchased in 2015.
The standard tax-free personal allowance for 2022/23 is £12,570.

Based solely on the facts above, what is the man's liability for income tax for 2022/2023?

A. £0.
B. £400.
C. £4,400.
D. £99.80.
E. £4,499.80.

19.14 Insolvency

42. A private limited company is a trade creditor of another company that has just entered administration. There are several creditors, both secured and unsecured.

Which of the following is correct about the statutory objectives of the administrator?

A. The administrator must attempt to rescue the company as a going concern.
B. The administrator must rescue the company as a going concern.
C. The administrator must only attempt to realise property for secured creditors.
D. The administrator is appointed by the floating charge holder so only needs to recover property secured by the floating charge.
E. The administrator is only responsible for returning money to unsecured creditors.

43. A client runs a small business that manufactures parts and sells them to a large engineering company that is a private limited company. The engineering company always pays very late and there are currently outstanding debts of £1,000. The engineering company's latest set of accounts state that it has annual profits of £10,000,000 and assets of £50,000,000. The client won a court action for the unpaid debt two months ago and has now served a statutory demand on the engineering company. The client has not heard anything from the engineering company for 24 days.

Is the client able to proceed with a winding-up petition against the company?

A. No, because the company is not insolvent according to the balance sheet test.
B. No, because there is no evidence that the company is insolvent.

C. Yes, because failing to pay the statutory demand means the company is deemed to be unable to pay its debts as they become due.
D. No, the client is unable to proceed because it would be a misuse of the winding-up process as the company is not insolvent and the client will incur expenses that he cannot recover.
E. No, the client cannot proceed until 28 days after the statutory demand has been served.

44. A private limited company has entered into the following loan agreements:

1. £100,000 borrowed from Bank A. The company granted the bank a floating charge over its whole undertaking on 21 August 2018. The charge was not registered.
2. £200,000 borrowed from Bank B. The company granted the bank a floating charge over its whole undertaking on 20 January 2020, and the charge was registered on 30 January 2020. Bank B was aware of the earlier charge granted to Bank A.
3. £100,000 borrowed from Bank C. The company granted a floating charge over its whole undertaking on 1 December 2020, and the charge was registered on 14 December 2020

Which of the banks, if any, will have priority in the event of a winding up?

A. None of the banks will have priority as they all have floating charges.
B. None of the banks will have priority because the rule of *pari passu* will apply.
C. Bank A will have priority as its floating charge was created first and Bank B had notice.
D. Bank C will have priority because its floating charge was registered earliest.
E. Bank B will have priority because its floating charge is registered, and the charge was granted earlier than Bank C.

45. A winding-up petition of a private limited company was announced in the *London Gazette* last week. A client is an unsecured creditor, and he spots the petition. The client knows that the company has £500,000 of assets remaining and that unusually there are no secured creditors (including floating charge holders). There is an outstanding debt of £100,000 to be paid to HMRC and also a small number of employees who have not been paid for the last month. The client is owed £100,000 out of total debts of £1,000,000. The client is hoping that he will receive £50,000 in the winding-up. The client's debt is the earliest of all the creditors.

Is the client likely to receive £50,000?

A. Yes. As the remaining assets will be divided amongst the creditors according to the proportion of the debt that they are owed.
B. No. The employees and HMRC are preferential creditors, and they take priority. There will also be the expenses of the winding up.
C. No. The client will receive £100,000 as his claim takes priority because it is the earliest.
D. Yes. Unsecured creditors usually receive 50% of their money in a winding up.
E. No, as there are preferential creditors. As an unsecured creditor, however, he will benefit from the top-slicing provisions, and this should enhance the amount he does receive.

46. A freelance musician has decided to apply for bankruptcy. He is aware that most of his remaining assets will be vested in the trustee in bankruptcy. He is particularly concerned that he will lose one asset, a valuable antique violin which the musician purchased with a personal unsecured bank loan five years ago.

Which of the following decisions is the trustee in bankruptcy most likely to make with regard to the violin?

A. The violin would be sold, and the proceeds would all go to the bank who originally lent the money.
B. The violin would be considered a "tool of the trade" and the musician will probably be able to keep it; however, it is possible that it may need to be replaced with a cheaper violin.
C. The musician will be allowed to keep the violin as it falls within the "cultural value" exception in the *Insolvency Act 1986*.
D. The violin will be sold, and all the proceeds will be distributed to the creditors.
E. Property in the violin will be vested in the trustee in bankruptcy who must sell it within three years, otherwise the violin must be returned to the musician.

47. A man is about to apply for bankruptcy. He is aware that his property will vest in the trustee in bankruptcy, and he is concerned about what will happen with the family home. The man has a wife and three children who are aged four, eight, and nine, all of whom live at the family home. The man and his wife are co-owners of the home and are joint tenants.

Advise the man if his family can continue to live at the family home.

A. Property vests in the trustee in bankruptcy immediately and the family can be evicted within 21 days.
B. The family can live in the house until all the children are 16.
C. The family can live in the house until all the children are 18.
D. The trustee in bankruptcy can seek a court order to sell the home; however, this is unlikely to happen for at least 12 months.
E. The matrimonial home does not form part of the assets vested in the trustee in bankruptcy.

20 Multiple-choice answers

20.1 Chapter overview

The following answers relate to the questions in the previous chapter. They are produced in a separate chapter to enable you test yourselves prior to checking the answers.

20.2 Business organisations

1. **B is the correct answer as the client is concerned about personal liability and wants the business to grow. A private limited company offers the shareholders limited liability and the corporate form has many advantages when it comes to raising capital.** A is incorrect as a partnership isn't always the most cost-effective option. C is incorrect because the client may need to submit tax accounts. D is incorrect as ordinary partnerships do not have a separate legal personality. E is incorrect. A limited company may be better for tax reasons, but this is not invariably the case.
2. **B is the correct answer. Shareholders are not responsible for the day-to-day running of the company, but they are required to make important decisions, either by the articles of association or the *Companies Act 2006*. Shareholders can be awarded dividends out of profits.** A is incorrect, although shareholders can be employees they are not required to be. C is incorrect as shareholders do not owe fiduciary duties to the company. D is incorrect as shareholders can influence the decision making of the company. E is incorrect as shareholders do not receive salaries but can be paid dividends.

20.3 Formation of the company

3. **A is correct. It is likely that limited liability will mean that he cannot be sued for debts of the business in the business fails; however, it is possible that liability could be imposed, for example under some of the provisions of the *Insolvency Act 1986*.** B is incorrect because it is not impossible for liability to be imposed. C is incorrect as the shareholder has limited liability, not the company. D is incorrect as the client's liability is limited. E is incorrect. It is common for directors and

DOI: 10.4324/9781003289760-26

officers to have insurance, but this is not what is meant by limited liability in this context.

4. **D is correct. It is possible, although unlikely, for a parent company to owe a tortious duty of care to the employee of a subsidiary company.** A is incorrect. The single economic unit doctrine is no longer supported by case law. B is incorrect. Although the client was not employed by the parent company, a tortious duty of care can still arise. C is incorrect. Although an agency relationship is possible, it is far from clear that one exists here. E is incorrect as the courts will not pierce the corporate veil just to satisfy a nebulous idea of justice.
5. **B is correct. Where someone makes contracts with another purporting to be on behalf of a company that has not yet been registered, that person will be bound by the contract unless there is an agreement to the contrary.** A and C are incorrect as the company was not yet in existence. D is incorrect, although the company could take on the contract. E is incorrect as there is no such clause in the model articles.
6. **B is correct. Where someone makes contracts with another purporting to be on behalf of a company that has not yet been registered, that person will be bound by the contract unless there is an agreement to the contrary.** A is incorrect as the company was not in existence. C is incorrect as the company was not in existence; also, even if there had been an agency relationship then liability would have been with the company as principal. D is incorrect as the liability will date from the time of the contract when the company was not in existence. E is incorrect. The multinational firm should have done this, but this does affect whether the client can be sued.

20.4 Constitution of the company

7. **C is the correct answer. The articles are a statutory contract and shareholders can enforce personal rights directly affecting their shares.** A is incorrect because rights stated in the articles cannot always be enforced by shareholders. B is incorrect because shareholders can sue in some situations. D is incorrect as rights can be enforced by other means, for example through an unfair prejudice petition. E is incorrect as management rights cannot be directly enforced through the articles.
8. **A is correct. A shareholders' agreement is a private contract between some or all shareholders.** B is incorrect as it does not need to be registered at Companies House. C is incorrect as it does not have to be with all shareholders and cannot bind past shareholders unless they sign up to it. It can only be amended by unanimous agreement unless alternative provisions are agreed in the shareholders' agreement. D is incorrect. The articles of association are compulsory. E is incorrect as it is not filed at Companies House.
9. **B is correct. MA14 can be disapplied by ordinary resolution.** A is incorrect as an ordinary resolution is sufficient. C is incorrect as removal is not necessary. D is incorrect as this would be a breach of duty. E is incorrect as the board does

not have the power to approve the transaction as they do not have the required quorum.

20.5 Roles in the company

10. **D is the correct answer because the board have the power to remove the company secretary. The company needs to inform Companies House.** A is incorrect as it refers to the procedure needed to remove a director or an auditor. B, C, and E are incorrect as the board has the power.

20.6 Financing the company

11. **B is the correct answer. Loan capital would mean that the client's share of the company is not diluted. As the company owns substantial fixed assets this may mean that a secured loan at a competitive rate can be negotiated with a lender.** A is incorrect because the company can grant a security over the machinery. C is incorrect because they have disagreed in the past and issuing more shares to the other director's husband may mean that the client loses control over the company. E is incorrect as the client will be entitled to a smaller proportion of future profits if her shareholding is diluted.
12. **A is the correct answer. The board have the power to allot shares but would need to give existing shareholders first refusal because of their pre-emption rights. These rights can be disapplied by special resolution. (It is possible that the shareholders could sign a deed waiving their rights, but the special resolution is probably more straightforward.)** B is incorrect as the power is often restricted. C is incorrect as it ignores the pre-emption rights. D is incorrect because shareholder approval is not needed in many circumstances. E is incorrect as the point about class rights is not relevant here.
13. **A is the correct answer. A shareholder with a 30% shareholding will be able to prevent the special resolution that is required to disapply the pre-emption rights.** B is incorrect as a special resolution is required. C is incorrect as the board does not have the power to disapply the pre-emption rights. D is incorrect as there is nothing to suggest a breach of this duty on the facts. E is incorrect. Although it is possible to waive the rights, they can also be disapplied by special resolution.

20.7 Shareholders' decision-making

14. **A is the correct answer. An ordinary resolution is required.** B is incorrect. A special resolution is not required and, in any event, there is no evidence that the other directors have a conflict of interest. C is incorrect as a court order is not required. D is incorrect as shareholder approval is needed. E is incorrect as

shareholder approval is needed and, in any case, the client does not have sufficient shares to guarantee an ordinary resolution.

15. **B is correct. As the client holds less than 5% of the shares, he cannot require the board to call a general meeting**. A is incorrect as the shareholder needs to have 5% of the voting shares. C is incorrect as he does not hold this proportion of shares. D is incorrect in the sense that the board can be required to call a meeting by shareholders. E is incorrect as the model articles do not stipulate this.

20.8 Directors' decision-making

16. **D is correct. The power to remove a company secretary rests with the board.** A, B, C, and E are incorrect as shareholder approval is not required.
17. **D is correct. Under MA 14 directors with a conflict of interest cannot vote or be counted in the quorum unless the MA14 is disapplied by ordinary resolution. If a disapplication does not happen, there are still two directors who can fulfil the quorum requirement who would both have to agree for the board resolution to be passed.** A is incorrect because the requirements of MA14 are in addition to the requirement to declare actual and potential conflicts of interest. B is incorrect as the client cannot be counted in the quorum. C is incorrect as the required quorum is two directors. E is incorrect as the quorum is two and the client cannot count in the quorum.

20.9 Directors' duties

18. **C is the correct answer. Breaches of the duty to exercise power for a proper purpose have often involved attempts to alter voting majorities by manipulating share capital**. A is incorrect as breaches of other duties are possible even if the board are seeking to promote the success of the company. B is incorrect. Although the board has got the power to allot shares, it may not be exercising its powers for a proper purpose. D is incorrect. The board are acting honestly and appear to be seeking to promote the success of the company. E is incorrect. There appears to be no indication of a conflict.
19. **B is the correct answer. The client must disclose the nature and extent of his interest to the board.** A is incorrect as liability for the conflict duties does not rely on honesty or good faith. C is incorrect. The duty to avoid conflicts is a subtly different duty and, in any event, ratification can only be done by the shareholders. D is incorrect as it does not need to be at a general meeting. E is incorrect as there is clear possibility of a conflict.
20. **C is the correct answer. The director has an interest in an existing transaction with the company which he must disclose to the board at the earliest opportunity.** A is incorrect as he must declare the interest now that he is aware. B is incorrect as the duty to avoid conflicts is a subtly different duty. D is incorrect as it is an existing transaction. He is unlikely to already be in breach of the duty to declare an interest in a proposed transaction because he was unaware

of the transaction and due to his illness, it would be unreasonable to expect him to have been aware. E is incorrect as disclosure can and should be made to the board.

21. **C is the correct answer. Directors owe their duties to the company, and it is for the company to sue. Shareholders can bring actions in some circumstances.** A is incorrect as shareholders can sometimes bring actions. B is incorrect because the board can decide to bring an action. D is incorrect as shareholders can bring an action sometimes. E is incorrect as the company can bring an action and shareholders can also bring an unfair prejudice petition.
22. **C is correct. Of those entitled to vote, 60% are happy to support the board so this is sufficient for the ordinary resolution required.** A is incorrect. The board does not have the power to ratify the breach. B is incorrect. Ratification requires an ordinary resolution only. D and E are incorrect as the breach can be ratified.
23. **C is correct. The client is in breach of his duty to act within the constitution, but this does not mean that the contract is voided, and the company may well still be bound.** A, B, and E are incorrect as the client still has the power to bind the company. D is incorrect. The client can still be in breach if the director has acted honestly.

20.10 Transactions with directors requiring shareholder approval

24. **B is the correct answer as this is a substantial property transaction.** A is incorrect as it is the value of the net assets that matter. C is incorrect because shareholder approval is not always needed, providing disclosure is made to the board. D is incorrect because it is an ordinary resolution that is required. E is incorrect. Property includes machinery.
25. **B is correct. This is a substantial property transaction because it is a property transaction over £100,000 with a connected person.** A is incorrect because the value is over £100,000 – in any event the percentage of net profits is not relevant to whether a transaction is a substantial property transaction. C is incorrect. A disclosure to the board will be necessary to avoid a breach of duty but additional approval by the shareholders is needed for a substantial property transaction. D is incorrect as the conflict of interest can be declared to the board. E is incorrect because the transaction is over £100,000 and with a connected person, so it is a substantial property transaction requiring approval by the shareholders.
26. **A is the correct answer. As the loan is over £10,000 it needs to be approved by the shareholders with an ordinary resolution.** B is incorrect as an ordinary resolution is required. C is incorrect as a court order is not required. D is incorrect as the board does not have the power to approve a loan of this size. E is incorrect. Even if the shareholder were permitted to vote on the matter, he does not have a majority of the shares.
27. **A is the correct answer. The termination clause means that it is not a long-term service contract that requires shareholder approval.** B, C, and E are incorrect as

it is not a long-term service contract. D is incorrect as shareholder approval is required for long-term service contracts.

28. **A is the correct answer as an ordinary resolution is required.** B is incorrect as it is not a small payment as it is over £200. C is incorrect as the model articles do not contain an exemption. D is incorrect as an ordinary resolution is sufficient. E is incorrect as it can also be authorised in a written resolution.

20.11 Minority shareholder protection

29. **A is the correct answer. The main advantage of the unfair prejudice petition is that can give a wronged shareholder an exit route out of the company, which means that a purchase of the shareholder's shares is usually the order made.** B is a possible remedy but not as common as A. C and D are theoretically possible but less likely than A. E is incorrect. A just and equitable winding-up order can be sought at the same time as an unfair prejudice petition, but this seems unlikely, based on the fact that the other directors are operating well together and could continue to be profitable. Also, it seems unlikely that the prejudiced shareholder will gain any more from this route.

20.12 Partnerships

30. **C is the correct answer.** A and E are incorrect as there is no requirement to be a qualified solicitor or accountant. B is incorrect as they do not have unlimited liability. D is incorrect as they are not nominated by Companies House, although they do have to be registered at Companies House.
31. **A is correct. Potentially the client could be liable for all the debts of the business.** B and D are incorrect. Irrespective of the agreements that the partners have made amongst themselves, the creditors can sue all or any one of the partners for the debts. C is incorrect as a partnership does not have separate legal personality. E is incorrect. This is the case with limited companies.
32. **B is correct. As the contract was made after the client left the partnership, liability may have been avoided providing notice requirements have been met and the client has not held herself out (or allowed herself to be held out) as a partner since retiring.** C is incorrect because liability is not inevitable after a partner has left. D is incorrect as it is not an LLP as it has not been registered at Companies House. E is incorrect as liability is not inevitable once a partner has left.
33. **C is correct. Under the *Partnership Act 1890* profits will be divided equally if there is no express or implied agreement to the contrary.** A, B, and E are incorrect as profits will be divided equally unless contracted otherwise. D is incorrect. There is no indication that the nephews are in breach, as they have not stipulated how much they will work in a partnership agreement.

34. A is correct. **As the partnership agreement is silent on this matter, the default rules of the *Partnership Act 1890* apply, and they stipulate that a change to the partnership agreement must be unanimous unless agreed otherwise in the partnership agreement.** B, C, and D are all incorrect because this decision must be unanimous. E is incorrect because most partnership decisions are by majority.
35. B is the correct answer. **As there is nothing in the partnership agreement about removal of a partner, the default rule is that the partner cannot be removed.** A, C, D, and E are all correct because no majority of the partners can remove another partner.
36. B is the correct answer. **The default rules are that most decisions can be taken by majority except for the introduction of a new partner, a change in the nature of the partnership business, or a change to the partnership agreement. The decision to employ the marketing director does not involve one of these exceptions.** A is incorrect as it relates to an expansion of the business not a change in the nature of the business. C and D are incorrect as a decision to take on staff can be made by a majority of the partners. E is incorrect. Although an ordinary partnership does not have a legal personality there can still be employees who are employed by those partners who are in position at the time of the employment.

20.13 Business accounts and tax

37. C is the correct answer. **Additions of £550,000 in the period are covered by the AIA of £1 million. WDA allowance = 18% of £2,370,500 = £426,690 add both AIA of £550,000 and WDA of £426,690 = £976,690.**
38. A is the correct answer. **TWDV b/f £2,370,500. Capital allowance for the year = £426,690. TWDV c/f = £1,943,810 (£2,370,500 - £426,690).**
39. E is the correct answer.

Sales (chargeable income)	**£1,645,000**
Less deductible expenditure:	
wages and salaries	**£602,000**
materials	**£200,500**
power, heat, light, and water	**£78,000**
rent and insurance	**£45,000**
Trading profit	**£719,500**

The sale of the fixed asset is not relevant to trading profit and will be taken as a chargeable capital gain if a profit on disposal has been achieved.

40. **C is correct. The trader will be required to make an adjusted tax payment.** A and B are incorrect as the GAAR does not impose direct criminal liability, although this can happen through failure to pay an adjusted tax demand. D is incorrect as the procedure is to make an adjusted tax demand. E is incorrect as there is no written warning procedure.
41. **A is the correct answer. The £10,000 profit from the one-off sale will not count as income. The £12,250 is below the personal allowance. The man is entitled to the saver starter rate so will pay £0 on his savings income. The dividend allowance is £2,000 so no tax is owed.**

20.14 Insolvency

42. **A is the correct answer. This is the overriding objective of administration. Although in many cases it will not be achieved, the administrator must attempt to rescue the company as a going concern.** B is incorrect as it is often not possible. C is incorrect. Although realising property for one or more secured or preferential creditors is an objective, the administrator must first attempt to rescue the company as a going concern, or then achieve a better result for the company's creditors as a whole than would be likely if the company were wound up. D is incorrect. Although a qualifying floating charge holder can appoint an administrator, the administrator has the same objectives as those referred to above. E is incorrect. The administrator as its objectives refer to all creditors.
43. **C is correct. Failure to pay the statutory demand is evidence of insolvency that can support a winding-up petition. The engineering company has not paid within 21 days so a petition can be commenced.** A and B are incorrect as the statutory demand is sufficient. D is incorrect because it is possible. There are potential ethical issues here and the solicitor would need to be certain that it was in the client's best interests because the costs of bringing a petition can be large. E is incorrect as the creditor has 21 days to pay.
44. **E is the correct answer. Bank B's charge was registered and was created first.** A is incorrect as the first registered charge will take priority. B is incorrect as registered charges are an exception to the principle of *pari passu*. C is incorrect as Bank A's charge was not registered. D is incorrect because Bank B's charge was created first.
45. **B is the correct answer. Although there are no secured creditors, HMRC and the employees are preferential creditors who have a higher priority. The expenses of a winding up are also significant so this will decrease the amount that can be distributed to unsecured creditors.** A is incorrect as even though this would work out on a strict application of the *pari passu* principle, insolvency law stipulates that other priorities get in the way. C is incorrect. The date of the claim is irrelevant as the unsecured creditors are deemed equal. D is incorrect as unsecured creditors will very rarely recover a large proportion of their debts in a winding up.

E is incorrect as the top-slicing provisions do not apply here as there are no floating charge holders.

46. **B is the correct answer as insolvent individuals are permitted to keep "tools of the trade". In this instance there could be a question of whether it is necessary for the musician to have an instrument of that value or whether a cheaper alternative would suffice.** A is incorrect. The bank which lent the money would have no proprietary claim to the proceeds and the loan was unsecured. If money is still owed to the bank in question, there will simply be another unsecured creditor for that debt. C is incorrect as there is no such exception. D is incorrect as the violin is a tool of the trade. E is incorrect. The three-year time limit relates to the family home.
47. **D is correct. The family home is vested in the trustee in bankruptcy; however, a court order is required to evict the family, and this is unlikely for 12 months. After that time, the creditors rights are deemed to outweigh any others and an eviction is much more likely.**

21 Problem scenarios

21.1 Chapter overview

The following exercises are designed to reflect the content of many of the areas discussed in previous chapters. The scenarios are not intended as SQE exam practice questions, but their style is influenced by the requirements of the SQE2 assessments.

21.2 Drafting exercise – incorporation of a company

The following exercise will give you experience of completing the IN01 form. All company forms are available on the Companies House website. After you have completed the form, you can compare your form with the completed form on the companion website.

From: Partner
Sent: November XX 2021
To: Trainee
Subject: Phil and John

Phil and John are two new clients who would like to incorporate their business as a private limited company. I need you to download and fill in the IN01 form. The following information should help.

- The articles will be the model articles with the amendments that you suggested.
- The address of the registered office will be: The Old Bakery, Worcester WR1 1A.
- Phil and John will be the only directors.
- Phil Anthony's and John Raby's service address with be the Old Bakery.
- There will not be a company secretary.
- Phil's home address is 1 Bun Hill, Worcester WR10 9A.
- John's home address is 2 Bun Hill, Worcester WR10 9A.
- Phil and John will hold one ordinary share each; this will have a nominal value of £1 and will be fully paid up.

DOI: 10.4324/9781003289760-27

21.3 Writing and drafting exercise – drafting the articles

From: Partner
Sent: November XX 2021
To: Trainee
Subject: Phil and John

Yesterday I met with two new clients, Phil Anthony and John Raby. Phil and John have run a very profitable bakery business together for 15 years now. The business is run as an ordinary partnership with Phil and John as the only partners. I was initially quite concerned to hear that there is no written partnership agreement, but it seems that this hasn't been a problem so far. Phil and John have decided that they want to expand their business and open two new bakery stores. Phil and John have decided that they want to change their business to run through a private limited company and are planning to finance the expansion with a mixture of equity and debt.

I have explained to Phil and John some of the requirements of incorporation and how the new company will need articles of association that will regulate the running of the company. I recommended that they adopt the model articles for private limited companies but also make amendments where necessary to meet their needs.

Although I think that the model articles will mostly work, we may need to make amendments to cater for the following concerns that Phil and John have:

- Phil and John are concerned that if they issue shares to other people they may lose control of the company and this may mean that they could be excluded from management. They would like a clause in the articles that can protect them from being removed as directors.
- Phil and John each have a variety of interests in the bakery trade and quite often form contracts with other businesses that they hold personal interests in. This doesn't cause any problems at present because they both fully disclose their personal interests. They do want to make sure that can participate fully in the decision-making on future contracts so please make sure that the articles will not impede this.
- Over the past ten years, Phil and John have changed the name of their trading business on three different occasions, largely to follow market trends on the high street. Although they do not currently have plans to change the company's name, they would like the flexibility to do this as easily as possible if they need to.

Please can you do the following:

1. Design a set of articles that:
   - Incorporate the model articles.
   - Exclude provisions of the model articles that conflict with Phil and John's wishes.
   - Include any new provisions that you consider will meet Phil and John's concerns.
2. Draft a letter for Phil and John, explaining why you have drafted the articles in this way and how the new articles meet their concerns.

21.4 Case and matter analysis/legal writing exercise – financing a new company

From: Partner
Sent: November XX 2021
To: Trainee
Subject: Brian and Phyllis

Yesterday I met with two new clients, Brian and Phyllis. They have just started selling chocolate that they make at their respective homes at a market stall. The chocolate has been very popular, and customers have placed advance orders for the next six months. They are struggling to keep up with demand and realise that they need to rapidly organise their business so they can expand.

Brian and Phyllis appear to be running their business as an ordinary partnership. I was initially quite concerned to hear that there is no written partnership agreement, but it seems that this hasn't been a problem so far. Brian and Phyllis have decided that they want to change their business to run through a private limited company because I suggested that this might be easier to raise capital. They have two investors, William and Mary, who are keen to invest £200,000 in the business and Brian and Phyllis hope that this will mean that they can take out a lease on premises in the high street. William and Mary have sent a proposal of how they would like to buy shares in the company.

Brian and Phyllis would like us to guide them through the incorporation process of the new company and would like advice on how to involve William and Mary in the company. They are particularly concerned about the following:

- They are concerned that they potentially lose control of the business in the future if William and Mary hold most of the shares.
- They would both like to be directors of the company and would like to protect their positions in the future.

Please draft a letter advising Brian and Phyllis that considers the proposal of William and Mary to invest in the company. You will need to address the advantages and disadvantages of the proposal and suggest alternatives if there are any.

21.5 Case and matter analysis/legal writing – share buyback

Memo from senior partner:

I met with a new client today called Fred Boyle. Fred is a shareholder and Managing Director in BMotors Ltd. There are three other directors who are also shareholders in the company.

Fred would like some advice on a buyback of shares from a retiring director, Morris Jupp. Morris is on good terms with his fellow directors, but he has decided he just wants to retire from business and realise his investment in the company. The remaining directors are not able to buy Morris's shares themselves so Morris has asked if the company itself can buy his shares, which have been independently valued at £110,000. Most of the shareholders are happy with the plan in theory, but they are concerned that one of the shareholders, Bryn Bowen, is not supportive and might seek to challenge the buyback.

BMotors Ltd was incorporated in 2014 with the model articles which have not been amended. The directors are Fred, Morris, Gavin, and Stacey. There are five shareholders who hold the following ordinary shares:

Issued share capital of BMotors Ltd

Shareholder	Shares issued	Nominal share value
Fred	10	£10
Morris	10	£10
Gavin	20	£20
Stacey	20	£20
Bryn	40	£40

Please can you draft a letter advising Fred about the buyback, whether it is possible, and if so, any procedures that the company may need to do to put it into effect.

21.6 Case and matter analysis – directors' duties

Read the following scenario that is based on the directors' general duties under the *Companies Act 2006*. Under each section there are key points worth considering.

Until recently, Ambrose, Bartholomew, Shannon, and Rishi were all directors of Fairwayextreme Ltd, a company providing adventure holidays in exotic locations. The company was incorporated in 2016 with the model articles with no amendments. Rishi is concerned about the following recent events.

Ambrose recently suggested in a board meeting that Fairwayextreme Ltd should enter a partnership with a new agency in Guatemala that specialised in sky-diving holidays. This was voted down by the board who felt that it was something that Fairwayextreme probably did not have the money to invest in at that time, so they did not want to take the risk. They also felt that the agency was quite a strong competitor for Fairwayextreme and were reluctant to have too close a link. Rishi has just heard that Ambrose, who resigned as director last week, has independently entered a contract with the Guatemalan agency and has received an advance commission of £50,000.

Consider:

- Is there an actual or potential conflict of interest here?
- Is there a breach even if Ambrose is no longer a director?
- Is it relevant that Fairwayextreme Ltd turned down the opportunity?
- Is it relevant that Fairwayextreme Ltd has not made a loss?
- Is there any evidence of authorisation?

21.7 Case and matter analysis – directors' duties

Bartholomew, another board member, is a very close friend of Sally who owns 30% of the shares in Fairwayextreme Ltd. Sally is not a registered director, but she does contribute lots of ideas and guidance to Bartholomew, which he often relays at board meetings. She also often sends Bartholomew memos on how to vote on board resolutions. Recently, following Sally's advice, the board decided to embark on a new venture with a kayaking company in Equatorial Guinea. The board relied on Sally because of her experience in the African travel business and invested heavily in the venture despite warnings in various trade journals that the kayaking business in Equatorial Guinea was becoming saturated and firms were going out of business. Rishi has just heard that the kayaking business has gone into liquidation owing Fairwayextreme Ltd £100,000. Rishi is also annoyed to discover that Sally was a shareholder and director of the kayaking company.

Consider:

- Although Sally is not a registered director, is she a *de facto* director and does she owe directors' duties?
- Are Bartholomew and the board exercising their independent judgement?
- Have the board exercised due diligence?
- Which of the conflict duties are engaged here?
- Is there any evidence of authorisation?

21.8 Case and matter analysis/ legal writing – partnership agreements

From: Partner
To: Trainee
Date: xx/03/2022
Subject: Francois & Bertram
XXXX

A new client, Francois came to see me this morning. Francois is in business with his friend Bernard, and they have been trading from a patisserie stall in the Worcester Market. All seems to be going very well and the new venture seems to be very profitable. They have been trading for six months now. They thought they may need some advice because they have not organised the business on a formal basis; it isn't registered anywhere, and they don't even have a written agreement about how it should be run. I found this a little alarming at first, but it seems that the lack of formality hasn't caused many problems so far. Francois has contributed 75% of the start-up capital and they have agreed that Bertram will take on more responsibilities with the running of the partnerships

I have explained to Francois that he and Bernard should have a written agreement that governs how they run their business as this could protect their interests in the long term. I told them that now their partnership was governed by the default rules in the *Partnership Act 1890* and although these may be OK for now, they may not be suitable in the long term.

Please can you draft a letter for me which I can send to Francois, explaining about the need for a written partnership agreement, indicating what sort of clauses might be suitable in this instance.

Index

For Product Safety Concerns and Information please contact our
EU representative GPSR@taylorandfrancis.com Taylor & Francis
Verlag GmbH, Kaufingerstraße 24, 80331 München, Germany